CROSSING UNDER COVER

Covered Bridges of Chester County, Pennsylvania,
and Surrounding Regions

(Including Cecil County, Maryland, and New Castle County, Delaware)

CROSSING UNDER COVER

Covered Bridges of Chester County, Pennsylvania,
and Surrounding Regions

(Including Cecil County, Maryland, and New Castle County, Delaware)

Sara Beth A. R. Kohut

SCHIFFER
PUBLISHING

4880 Lower Valley Road • Atglen, PA 19310

Other Schiffer Books on Related Subjects:

Bridges of Lancaster County, **Bruce M. Waters**, ISBN: 978-0-7643-3427-6

Pennsylvania's Covered Bridges: A Keepsake, **Michael P. Gadomski**, ISBN: 978-0-7643-6604-8

Timeless Crossings: Vermont's Covered Bridges, **Michael J. McCormack**, ISBN: 978-0-7643-3830-4

Unless otherwise noted, all photographs are provided courtesy of Jim and Gloria Smedley or the Theodore Burr Covered Bridge Society of Pennsylvania, Inc.

Type set in Lust Text/Montserrat

ISBN: 978-0-7643-6750-2
Printed in China

Published by Schiffer Publishing, Ltd.
4880 Lower Valley Road
Atglen, PA 19310
Phone: (610) 593-1777; Fax: (610) 593-2002
Email: info@schifferbooks.com
Web: www.schifferbooks.com

For our complete selection of fine books on this and related subjects, please visit our website at www.schifferbooks.com. You may also write for a free catalog.

Schiffer Publishing's titles are available at special discounts for bulk purchases for sales promotions or premiums. Special editions, including personalized covers, corporate imprints, and excerpts, can be created in large quantities for special needs. For more information, contact the publisher.

A tranquil spring scene at Hayes Clark Covered Bridge. *Photo courtesy of Jim and Gloria Smedley, ©2015*

The grave itself is but a covered bridge,
Leading from light to light,
through a brief darkness!

—Henry Wadsworth Longfellow

We build too many walls and
not enough bridges.

—Isaac Newton

TABLE OF CONTENTS

INTRODUCTION

For as long as I can remember, the mantel in my parents' living room featured a small postcard-size painting that stood on an equally minuscule easel. The painting depicts the Bell Bank Covered Bridge, its brilliant-red siding a striking contrast to the white snow on its roof and surrounding country landscape. That bridge stood across Octoraro Creek in Upper Oxford Township until I was a toddler. I don't personally remember that bridge, but my father kept it alive with his stories about attending Sunday school picnics on its banks and going on lazy-afternoon childhood ventures to swim underneath it. There is a romantic lore to covered bridges, so it is not lost on me that Bell Bank stood along the road my parents would have traveled to see each other when they were courting. Every time I looked at that painting, I thought it must have been something very special, since our home was not adorned with many pieces of original art.

Apparently, my father felt a connection to the area's covered bridges. One of my strongest childhood memories is of my father taking me to see the Jackson's Mill Covered Bridge in July 1985, after it had been swept off its foundation by a flood. I can still picture the beaten siding and exposed framework of the bridge as it rested awkwardly, like a desolate boat stranded after having run aground, on the muddy shore of the creek it was supposed to traverse. Even as an eight-year-old child, I could appreciate the forces of nature necessary to dislodge and move such an imposing structure as that. Fortunately, the powers that be decided to restore that bridge, and it still (as I write this piece) occupies a place of prominence fording Octoraro Creek.

Jackson's Mill Covered Bridge was swept off its foundation in a 1985 flood. In short order, it was rebuilt and still crosses Octoraro Creek. *Photo courtesy of Theodore Burr Covered Bridge Society of Pennsylvania, Inc., ©1985*

I was reminded of that experience on September 2, 2021, when my husband (not a native to the area) asked if there was a covered bridge nearby named Rudolph and Arthur. When I responded affirmatively, he informed me that someone on Twitter was reporting it had been washed away that day, a victim of the record-setting floods caused by the remnants of Hurricane Ida. Sure enough, a 5-mile drive brought me to the now-empty site of the covered bridge that had stood for 140 years. It was remarkable to see: the bridge was gone, simply vanished!

The space previously occupied by that connector was now a gaping hole. The stone-and-cement abutments stood naked on either side of what was now a very docile-looking branch of Elk Creek, its chocolate-colored waters gurgling happily between them. Mud-downed grass sprawled for dozens of feet around the roadway and the banks along the creek. Branches of all sizes and even whole trees and other debris lay strewn about in odd locations.

My eight-year-old son stood at the edge of the pier, enjoying the height over the waters, his feet steps away from what hours earlier had been the approach to the bridge.

"Where did the bridge go?" I pondered aloud. Other than the top portion of the portico, which had been deposited in the mud next to the abutment, there was no sign of it.

Rudolph & Arthur Covered Bridge in 2015. The Commonwealth of Pennsylvania had plans to rehabilitate the bridge before record-high floodwaters from the remnants of Hurricane Ida destroyed it on September 1, 2021. *Photo courtesy of Jim and Gloria Smedley, ©2015*

"Look at this! It's just gone!" I exclaimed.

"This is boring," my son replied, as he shuffled his feet through muddy pebbles.

But I stood in astonishment, stupefied as to how something of that size, that had stood for so long, could all of a sudden just be gone, nearly without a trace! It was the same sense of awe and wonder that I had felt as a child when I saw the carcass of Jackson's Mill Covered Bridge sitting on the opposite shore.

I dragged my apathetic son to see what was left of the two other covered bridges in Elk Township (they were not unscathed but survived because, unlike their neighbor, they had steel reinforcements). We ran into other bridge enthusiasts, one of whom informed me that we would find the remains of the Rudolph and Arthur bridge downstream.

Sure enough, lodged under a modern open crossing on Route 841 in an area called Springlawn, we could see pieces of the flooring, the siding, the roof, and several of the massive beams that had formed the structure of the Rudolph and Arthur bridge since 1880. Caught up in the wreckage was a mass of tall trees, likely downed and carried there by the floodwaters. Evidence of the height the deluge had reached was on clear display as more muddy debris and downed cornstalks marked a path hundreds of feet wider than the normal creek path.

What a sight it must have been when the bridge floated downstream! I can only wonder how long it stayed together before the various pieces broke apart. I visited that debris site several times over several weeks, equally fascinated and saddened by what I witnessed there. One can only hope that the bridge will be rebuilt in a way that pays homage to its predecessor.

I knew of the Rudolph and Arthur Covered Bridge not so much because I live locally to it, but because several years ago, I found myself in a place where I had the time and desire to research and write about items of historical interest in Chester County. I cannot recall the exact project I was working on, but something inspired me to check out the newspaper-clipping files of the Chester County Historical Society. There I found newspaper articles and brochures published decades ago on Chester County's covered bridges, usually containing a map, a driving tour, and summary descriptions of the spans.

Having grown up in southern Chester County, I took it for granted that there were covered bridges around. I knew of Pine Grove Covered Bridge and some others in Lancaster County, but other than that I knew surprisingly little about the covered bridges in our area. Frankly, I had heard more about Bell Bank Covered Bridge and its close neighbor Newcomer's Covered Bridge, both of which had crossed Octoraro Creek before they burned when I was a small child, than I did about the extant bridges. I had no clue there were three in Elk Township alone. Or that there were about a dozen more in the middle and northern sections of Chester County. Until starting my research, I did not appreciate that most of the bridges I frequently travel on back roads were once covered, and that we are one of the few communities today fortunate to have multiple covered bridges within a short driving distance.

Perhaps the seed was there from that tiny painting on my parents' mantel and the stories they told me a child, or maybe it was the universal appeal of these idyllic pastoral structures that inspires bridge "collectors" to travel the country in pursuit of them. Whatever the reason, I decided to try out some of those old covered-bridge tours and figure out which bridges still existed. What an adventure that was, using maps showing old route numbers and long-since-closed roads, and me not knowing whether there would still be a bridge standing should I even find my way to each location. In the process of discovering the covered bridges, I saw a lot of Chester County that I had never seen before and learned a great deal of local history.

We appreciate covered bridges for their scenic beauty today, but they originally served a practical purpose that was as important to the local economy as it was to transportation. Trust me, once you start to tour the covered bridges, you will only want to learn more about them and their communities. You will never look at a bridge the same and will start to notice the intricate features that distinguish one covered bridge from another. You may even find yourself (like me) taking back-road detours when you're on vacation to find covered bridges indicated on a road map.

It started out innocently enough as a personal quest to see the old bridges. From my childhood memories, through research and word of mouth, I learned of more and more local bridges. I found myself taking photographs of each bridge and writing down driving directions. Eventually, I produced an article on the covered bridges for the *Chester County Press*, where I worked for a short time as a staff writer. I had hoped the readers would consider it a keepsake, like the old ones I found at the historical society. Apparently, some did.

A few years after the *Press* article, I was approached about turning the article into a book. My researching, driving-tour testing, and photographing began anew, but then got waylaid for several years. By the time I picked the project up again (and until Ida swept through, damaging nearly every covered bridge in the area), all the bridges I had originally written about were still standing, and five had been rehabilitated or reconstructed. That is a happy contrast to most of the old articles in the historical society's files that deplored the condition of the bridges (with gaps in their siding and roofs, moss and grass covering their unstable floors, or worse) or noted the loss of bridges to fire, flood, neglect, or damage from overweight vehicles.

After delving into the history, legends, and lore of local covered bridges, it was hard not to develop a passion for them. Now it's practically a reflex to visit a new area of the country and wonder where the nearest covered bridge is located. And in moments of downtime or stuck-at-home time, I can visit Bell Bank bridge by looking at that postcard-size painting that used to stand on my parents' mantel but now occupies a shelf of honor in my home.

This book is intended to provide a factual guide and driving directions to the covered bridges in the greater Chester County area. I have included a few stringers as well, but because they are simple, modern structures, frequently within a residential development, I have not made an exhaustive effort to cover all the stringers in the area. I hope you enjoy reading about the covered bridges and find the time to get out and see them for yourself.

A COVERED-BRIDGE PRIMER

A General History of Covered Bridges

There is something magical about covered bridges. Literally and figuratively, they connect the past and the present. They are remnants from a bygone era that have stood the tests of time. Enthusiasm for them is contagious, as is nostalgia for those spans of which only ruins or photographs remain. Covered bridges become symbols of their community, tourist destinations, and reminders of earlier ways of life.

When the phrase "covered bridge" is mentioned, a lot of people think of New England, or perhaps even Iowa, made famous by the book and movie *The Bridges of Madison County*. But Pennsylvania has played an integral role in the history of covered bridges. In fact, the very first covered bridge in the United States was built in Pennsylvania.

Around 1798, a subscription company was organized to build a "Permanent Bridge" extending what is now Market Street across the Schuylkill River in Philadelphia. Construction was underway by 1801 and the bridge opened in 1803, but its covering was not complete until 1805. The company called in New England bridge builder Timothy Palmer to complete the protective wooden superstructure to ensure the span's longevity. Called the Permanent Bridge, the structure was 1,300 feet long (including the deck, abutments, and wing walls), had three spans, and accommodated two lanes of traffic. The cost of construction was $300,000. As a toll bridge, which most bridges were in those days, it brought in $13,000 during its first year. The City of Philadelphia sold the bridge in 1840, after which it was replaced with a wooden structure that could accommodate rail traffic that reportedly stood until destroyed by fire in 1875.

Pennsylvania was also home to the second covered bridge in America. Through five spans stretching more than 1,000 feet long, the bridge connected Morrisville, Pennsylvania, with Trenton, New Jersey. Its builder was Theodore Burr, who was born in Torrington, Connecticut, in 1771. He earned great prominence in Pennsylvania and created the structural design upon which nearly all the covered bridges in the Chester County region are constructed. Burr obtained a patent for his arch truss design in 1817. Because an 1836 fire destroyed many records at the United States Patent Office, only the drawing of his design survives. Burr received royalties from his patent and has been credited with building nearly fifty bridges by the time he died in 1822, although modern researchers have yet to verify that total. Despite his success, Burr had poorly managed his finances, and when he died, his estate lacked the resources for a proper burial, and he was interred in an unmarked grave.

The Keystone State also holds the record for the longest covered bridge built, which stretched for more than 1 mile over the Susquehanna River between Columbia, Lancaster County, and Wrightsville, York County. It was built in 1814 by Jonathan Walcott and consisted of twenty-eight spans. After an ice storm destroyed the bridge, it was rebuilt in 1834, only to be torched by Union soldiers in 1863 to stave off the approach of the Confederate army. The bridge was again rebuilt in 1868 but destroyed by a storm in 1896.

At one time, the United States had more than 14,000 covered bridges. Today, there are fewer than 900 (about 840 as of 2021, including some built in the past half century) (Pierce et al. 2005, 3; Caswell 2021, xii). Thirty states have at least one covered bridge, but Pennsylvania, the birthplace of the covered bridge, is the capital, with 209 covered bridges (Caswell 2021, xiv). Ohio is the only other state to have at least a hundred covered bridges (it has 144), with Vermont and Indiana close behind with ninety-six and ninety-two covered bridges, respectively (Caswell 2021, xiv).

An estimated more than 1,500 covered bridges once stood in Pennsylvania, with most having been built before the 1900s. All but three of the state's sixty-seven counties had at least one covered bridge. Currently, almost forty counties in Pennsylvania have at least one covered bridge. Chester County, with fourteen, has the fourth-highest number of covered bridges in Pennsylvania. Lancaster County is first with twenty-eight, while Washington County and Columbia County each have twenty-three. Among Chester County's other neighboring counties, Delaware County can claim only the intercounty bridge it shares with Chester County, Montgomery County has no covered bridges, and Berks County has five. Even Philadelphia County has one covered bridge: the Thomas Mill Covered Bridge over Wissahickon Creek in Fairmont Park.

Wooden covered bridges are not unique to the United States; they exist in Canada, China, Europe, Indonesia, Japan, Thailand, Vietnam, and South America. Some of the oldest covered bridges are located outside the United States.

Why Were the Bridges Covered?

At its most basic level, covering a bridge serves a utilitarian purpose. Bridges represented an improvement over fords, which could be treacherous to cross during floods and were expensive to build and maintain. Wood was a natural choice as a bridge-building material, and most covered bridges were built of locally available wood. In the Chester County area, pine was a popular choice because it was lightweight but sturdy, inexpensive, and plentiful as a resource. Wood, however, is vulnerable to fire, rot, and insects. Covering the bridge protects its floor, supports, and wooden peg joints from wet weather and scorching sun. An uncovered wooden bridge may last a few decades, but a covered wooden bridge may (as many have with maintenance) last well over a century.

Most bridges in rural areas were used by farmers to carry their goods to the mills and markets, so the covered structures had to be built large and strong enough to accommodate a loaded wagon. In winter snow, however, bridges were often "snowed" (snow was applied to the bridge's deck) to provide passage for sleighs. The covering could also provide solace to a weary traveler stuck in bad weather.

Another explanation often provided for covering the bridges is that it facilitated the herding of animals across the span. That explanation suggests that some animals were spooked by seeing their reflections in the water or perhaps by the elevation, notwithstanding that animals would have crossed open bridges for many centuries prior to the first walled-in crossings being built.

A third explanation is that most bridge builders were also barn builders, who employed the same construction techniques when building bridges. Many covered bridges do bear resemblance to barns, which could also have assuaged animals prone to fright. The barnlike appearance also would blend well with the surrounding aesthetics of a rural landscape.

An incidental benefit of the covering—privacy—gives rise to the nickname of "kissing bridges." Many a courting couple must have slowed their passage under the covering to steal a lover's kiss before the eyes of the open world were again upon them when they emerged on the other side. The covered passages are also called "wishing bridges," giving travelers a brief respite to make wishes as they cross. The covering also adds a layer of mystery that occasionally has given rise to legends of trolls and ghosts.

The wooden sides of a bridge often served as the billboards of their day. Chester County's Rapps Dam Covered Bridge once bore an insurance ad, while Bartram's Covered Bridge displayed a political slogan. The structures also bore signs of warnings or toll alerts. Many a covered bridge's portal warned travelers that they could be fined for smoking on the bridge or crossing their horses at a pace faster than a walk. The former could lead to destruction of the bridge by fire, while the latter was thought to cause damage to the bridge through heavy vibrations. Today, most covered bridges are posted with height and weight limit signs. However, there are too many stories of oversized trucks ignoring these signs and causing damage to the precarious structures of these bridges.

How Were Covered Bridges Named?

Most covered bridges in the Chester County region were named after a person or family who either owned nearby land or a local mill or held a prominent position in the community, such as postmaster. Because those persons or families were subject to change, the names of covered bridges were not usually static, and the changing names invariably led to confusion. In the early 1900s, Chester County tried to resolve the problem of erratic names by assigning every bridge (not just covered bridges) a number, starting with 1 in the southwestern corner up to 221 in the northeastern corner. That solution encountered some difficulty when neighboring Lancaster County numbered its bridges in the reverse direction.

The National Society for the Preservation of Covered Bridges, which publishes the *World Guide to Covered Bridges*, utilizes a numbering convention that originated with a covered-bridge group in Ohio (Caswell 2021, xv). This tripartite numbering system catalogs each bridge by its state, county, and sequence. Accordingly, Chester County covered bridges are identified first by the number 38 for Pennsylvania, then the number 15 for Chester County, followed by a third number indicating its sequence within the county. If the bridge has been rebuilt, a fourth number will be included. For example, the Hayes Clark bridge is identified as 38-15-07#2. The *World Guide* numbering system serves to distinguish bridges that have similar names but distinct locations.

Regardless of the formal identity number, most bridges, covered bridges included, are better known by their colloquial names. As may be expected, there often are variations in how specific bridge names are spelled. For example, in 2012, Pennsylvania's Bureau for Historic Preservation submitted additional documentation for the 1980 listing of the Linton Stevens Covered Bridge on the National Register of Historic Places, noting that further research had revealed that the structure's namesake spelled his name as Stephens. For consistency, this book uses the bridge names set forth in the *World Guide*.

What Happened to All the Covered Bridges?

There are several reasons why covered bridges have disappeared from our landscape. Their wooden structures do not always withstand the tests of time: storms, floods, fire, insects, rot, and the needs and stresses of modern travel. As the stories in the Chester County region demonstrate, storms frequently destroyed or damaged covered bridges. Floods, ice, and wind were often too much for a bridge to withstand, as was snow accumulation on a deteriorated roof. Storms in June 1884 destroyed or swept away several covered bridges in the area. Newspaper articles of the time reported that flooding from that storm knocked out nearly all the covered bridges on Octoraro and Elk Creeks, including thirteen in Chester and Lancaster Counties and seventeen in Cecil County, Maryland (Untitled, *Daily Local News*, January 18, 1885; July 14, 1884). Storm floods continue to wreak havoc on the old bridges, as the remnants of Hurricane Ida reminded us in September 2021.

Fire has destroyed many a wooden covered bridge and is another reason why many have been replaced with structures consisting of elements invulnerable to fire. Lightning strikes can be the culprit, but more often arson is to blame. Several of the Chester County–area covered bridges have been reconstructed with special kinds of African wood or other elements to make them resistant to fire. While African woods resistant to rot, insects, and fire seem a good selection for a long-lasting bridge, some think the use of those foreign hardwoods is inappropriate because it is inconsistent with the historical integrity of the original bridge, and the density of the wood puts greater strain on the structure than the original lightweight pine.

Over time, many covered bridges were replaced by modern structures constructed of iron, steel, concrete, or stone. As those designs became the norm, the cost of building and repairing wooden covered spans increased to the point that it often outweighed the benefits of maintaining a one-lane, high-maintenance structure designed to accommodate horse carriages and farm equipment from the nineteenth century. A lot of covered bridges have been reinforced with steel runners to improve their weight-carrying capacity, but they still cannot match the load-bearing ability of modern structures. Nor can they withstand the pressure when an oversize or overweight vehicle attempts to pass through the portals.

Equally as damaging to covered bridges as fire and storm damage is neglect. Maintenance and repair are important to any wooden structure, whether a house, barn, or other building. It is even more important to a bridge that crosses a body of water and must carry the weight of its crossers.

Perhaps the most dramatic end to a nearby covered bridge was that of the Upland Covered Bridge over Chester Creek in neighboring Delaware County. The span reportedly had a starring role in the 1915 movie *On Bitter Creek*, about lovers from feuding families that are separated by the crossing. In the climax of the movie, the bridge is blown up. However, symbolic of the relations between the families, the span is rebuilt. In reality, a movie company learned that the Upland bridge was fated for demolition, and was inspired to create a movie around the demolition and its replacement with a modern structure (Rathmell 1958, 9).

AN OVERVIEW OF THE COVERED BRIDGES OF CHESTER COUNTY AND SURROUNDING REGIONS

Of Chester County's fourteen covered bridges, three are intercounty connectors. Chester and Lancaster Counties share the Pine Grove and Mercer's Mill Covered Bridges over the Octoraro. At one point, the two counties shared ten covered bridges. On the east end of the county, Bartram's Covered Bridge connects Chester County with Delaware County. Historically, the costs for intercounty bridges were split between the two counties.

Chester County's covered bridges seem to be concentrated in several areas. Close to the Oxford area are Pine Grove and the bridges in Elk Township: Glen Hope, Linton Stevens, and Rudolph and Arthur (assuming it is rebuilt). The middle section of the county has Speakman No. 1 within a few miles of the Speakman No. 2 / Mary Ann Pyle and Hayes Clark Covered Bridges, which are on private property. A short drive north leads to Gibson's Covered Bridge outside Downingtown. Farther north, the Larkin's, Hall's/Sheeder's, Kennedy, Rapps Dam, and Knox Covered Bridges all are within a short distance of each other. A few stringers, or small, modern covered bridges lacking a truss, exist in various places, including two in the White Clay Creek Preserve that are included in this book.

The oldest covered bridge in Chester County is Hall's/Sheeder's, built in 1850. The longest is the two-span Pine Grove Covered Bridge, at 204 feet. The shortest is Larkin's Mill at 60 feet.

Although located in neighboring Lancaster County, the White Rock Forge and Jackson's Mill Covered Bridge are very close to Chester County. They cross the West Branch of the Octoraro, and their location between Pine Grove and Mercer's Mill makes for a convenient driving tour of four covered bridges.

Chester County's location in southeastern Pennsylvania puts it in proximity to the covered bridges in Cecil County, Maryland, and New Castle, Delaware. To area residents who (like the author) live close to the tristate line, the bridges in Maryland and Delaware are closer and easier to visit than those in northern Chester County, which is why they are included in this book.

Cecil County has two covered bridges, including one that came from a DuPont estate and one that underwent a much-needed major rehabilitation. Once the home of more than seventy covered bridges (including a ten-span crossing that was 1,700 feet long at Conowingo, and a dozen covered crossings over Big Elk, Little Elk, and North East Creeks), Maryland now has only six remaining.

Delaware was once home to more than 125 covered bridges. Today, it has only three remaining—Ashland, Smith's Bridge, and Wooddale—but the state has demonstrated a strong commitment to preserving its covered bridges. All three have been rebuilt or substantially rehabilitated in the past few decades, with the advocacy and support of citizens in the bridges' communities being fundamental. Absent the public demand, Delaware may very well have lost all of its covered bridges by now. Indeed, as I drove through Rolling Mill Road in search of Wooddale Covered Bridge in 2005, using an out-of-date driving tour, I was disappointed to find only remnants of the bridge. Given the rampant commercial development in New Castle County, I doubted the likelihood of the historic relic's return. When I began updating my research for this project, I was delighted to learn that the bridge not only had been rebuilt but had been reconstructed as a replica of the original, improved to withstand modern traffic and once-in-a-century floods, like the 2003 flood that destroyed the original. I should not have been surprised, however, given the state's decision to reconstruct Smith's Covered Bridge four decades after the original was destroyed by arson. Delaware also has a few stringer covered bridges in several residential developments.

GONE, BUT NOT FORGOTTEN

To the author, a book on Chester County covered bridges would seem incomplete without discussion of Bell Bank Covered Bridge. As indicated earlier, although Bell Bank has been gone for more than four decades, it left an indelible impression on the community. I have come to know Bell Bank Covered Bridge through paintings, photographs, and memories shared with me by family and friends. The bridge crossed Octoraro Creek on Street Road, the historic road that once ran from Market Street in Philadelphia to the Susquehanna River, between Upper Oxford Township in Chester County and Colerain Township in Lancaster County. The Burr arch structure was 112 feet long and 15 feet wide, with red horizontal siding and white portals. Built in 1850, the bridge was named for James Patterson Bell, a colonel in the Revolutionary War, who owned a mill and property near the bridge. Lightning burned the bridge in 1860, and it was rebuilt in 1861 for $1,739 by its original builder, Robert Russell.

Arsonists destroyed the bridge in March 1979, and an open modern structure replaced it. Apparently, citizen support for rebuilding the covered bridge was lacking then, but interest has resurfaced periodically over the years. Around 2010, several local residents formed a taskforce to investigate the possibility of a new covered bridge, using the State of Delaware's reconstruction of Smith's Bridge as a model. To date, those efforts have not resulted in the reconstruction of the bridge. Nonetheless, fondness for the long-lost span keeps its memory alive.

DISTINGUISHING THE COVERED BRIDGES

To a novice, covered bridges may all look the same. But a closer look reveals many distinguishing features:

Look at the entrance to the bridge—Are there parapets? Do they connect into the wing walls and abutments? Are they rounded, capped, or jagged? Do they curve around the bridge?

Look at the portal—What shape is it? What direction does the siding run?

Look at the side of the bridge—Which direction does the siding run?

Observe the color of the bridge—Is the siding painted or stained? Are the sides the same color as the portals? Is the interior of the bridge painted?

Look for windows—Are they at the end or the center of the bridge? Are they on both sides of the bridge? Are they big or small?

Look inside the bridge—Is there an arch? How high does the arch reach on the side of the bridge? Are there multiple arches? If so, are they stacked or end to end? Or does the structure resemble lattice?

Observe the placement of the bridge—Does the bridge cross straight over the water or at an angle? Is there a pier, or support, under the middle of the bridge?

Look at the floor—Are there strips of wood for vehicle wheels or not? Do the planks run lengthwise or crosswise?

Look for signs on the bridge—Is there one on the portal? In the parapets? On the interior of the bridge? Does the center post indicate a municipality border?

Keep these features in mind during your visits to the covered bridges, and you will no doubt discover that each bridge is unique and interesting in its own way.

GLOSSARY OF COVERED-BRIDGE TERMINOLOGY

abutment: The supports at the end of a bridge, usually built of stone or concrete. In the Burr arch truss, it often is where the end of the arch sits.

approach: The road as it leads into the bridge

deck: The floor of the bridge upon which traffic travels

parapet: Walls rising above the surface of the road at the end of a bridge, usually built of field stone. Sometimes they're like arms welcoming you into the bridge. Most of the Chester County covered bridges exhibit parapets made of fieldstone. The style predominates so much in the commonwealth that they are called "Pennsylvania parapets."

pier: A structure standing between the abutments, usually in the center of a bridge, often added to strengthen the support; usually made of stone, concrete, or steel

portal: The facade and opening at the entrance and exit of a bridge

runners: Supports that run lengthwise under the bridge

span: The length of the bridge between supports

stringer: A simple bridge, usually of a short span and lacking a true truss

truss: The structural frame of a bridge

wing wall: An extension of an abutment that acts as a retaining wall against the embankment. Sometimes it may extend into a parapet.

COVERED-BRIDGE STRUCTURES

In simple terms, the truss is the basic framework or structure of the bridge. As a technical matter, each bridge has two trusses, one on each side of the frame. All the covered bridges in Chester County are constructed on the basis of the Burr arch truss design, except for the Hayes Clark and Speakman No. 2, which are queen post truss bridges. The two covered bridges in Cecil County, Maryland, are also Burr arch truss bridges, as is Smith's Covered Bridge in Delaware. The Ashland and Wooddale Covered Bridges in Delaware have Town lattice truss structures. Other truss designs exist, but this section will focus only on the designs relevant to the bridges discussed in this book.

The King Post Truss

The oldest and simplest truss is the king post truss. It is composed of a vertical beam, called the king post, which in some instances is tapered. A diagonal beam leans against each side of the king post to form a right angle on either side. Additional posts and diagonals can be added in even numbers to support a longer span. The king post truss basically resembles a triangle with a center vertical line. Approximately ninety-five covered bridges, or 10 percent, in the United States are built of multiple king post trusses (Pierce et al. 2005, 40).

The bare frame of Lippencott / Cox Farm Covered Bridge, 38-36-25#3, in Greene County, Pennsylvania, exemplifies a single king post truss. *Photo courtesy of Jim and Gloria Smedley, ©2013*

Packsaddle Covered Bridge, 38-56-02, in Somerset County, Pennsylvania, is supported by multiple king post trusses. *Photo courtesy of Jim and Gloria Smedley, ©2020*

The Queen Post Truss

The queen post truss represents an expanded version of the king post truss. Instead of a single king post, two posts support a beam running lengthwise between them, while diagonal beams form right angles against each post. Essentially, the queen post resembles a rectangle on its side, with a right-angle triangle on either end. There are about a hundred extant queen post truss covered bridges in the United States (Pierce et al. 2005, 37).

The queen post truss is visible in the Hayes Clark Covered Bridge. *Photo courtesy of Jim and Gloria Smedley, ©2015*

The Burr Arch Truss

Theodore Burr's arch truss design combines a multiple king post truss with an arch running from below the truss into the abutment on each end. The arch beams sandwich the king post and its diagonal beams. The arch makes the structure stronger than the traditional king post truss, permitting a longer span. The Burr arch truss has proved to be one of the most resilient structures, with about 224 or 25% of remaining covered bridges exhibiting the construction (Pierce et al. 2005, 42).

Some bridges have multiple arches: they can be stacked to add further strength to a single span (usually no more than two arches stacked in a single span), or they can be laid end to end with one pier or more to support multiple spans.

The Burr arch truss features a king post truss combined with an arch. Some bridges feature a double or stacked arch, as shown here in Gilpin's Falls Covered Bridge and Rapps Dam Covered Bridge. *Photos courtesy of Jim and Gloria Smedley, ©2013 and 2015*

The Town Lattice Truss

The Town lattice truss essentially looks like latticework, with crisscrossing beams forming the framework of the bridge. The design is named for Ithiel Town, a contemporary of Burr and a fellow native of Connecticut. Town obtained a patent for the lattice truss in 1820. He reportedly charged bridge builders a royalty of $1 per foot to use his design. Compared to the king post, queen post, and Burr arch designs, which required large pieces of timber, the Town lattice truss utilized shorter pieces of lumber. The design was also more accessible to bridge builders with less developed skills. Town lattice truss covered bridges number about 135 (Pierce et al. 2005, 43).

The Town lattice truss can be seen in Wooddale Covered Bridge in Delaware. *Photo courtesy of Jim and Gloria Smedley, ©2013*

MAP OF COVERED BRIDGE LOCATIONS

Bridges on the Driving Tour:

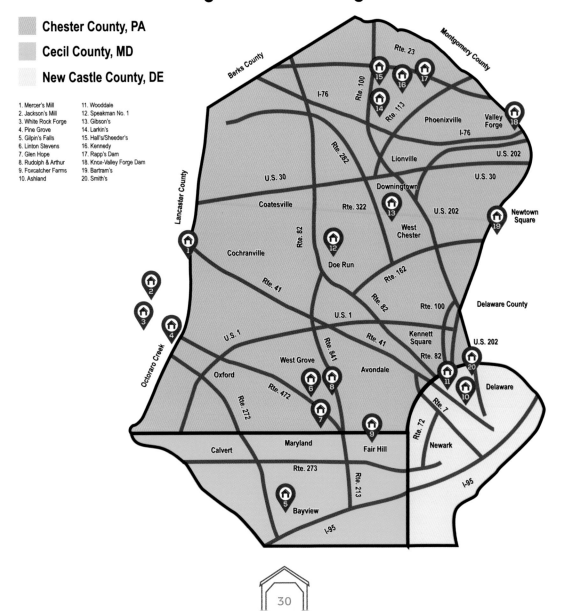

Chester County, PA
Cecil County, MD
New Castle County, DE

1. Mercer's Mill
2. Jackson's Mill
3. White Rock Forge
4. Pine Grove
5. Gilpin's Falls
6. Linton Stevens
7. Glen Hope
8. Rudolph & Arthur
9. Foxcatcher Farms
10. Ashland
11. Wooddale
12. Speakman No. 1
13. Gibson's
14. Larkin's
15. Hall's/Sheeder's
16. Kennedy
17. Rapp's Dam
18. Knox-Valley Forge Dam
19. Bartram's
20. Smith's

THE COVERED BRIDGES OF CHESTER COUNTY, PENNSYLVANIA

Bartram's Covered Bridge

Also Known as: County Bridge #159; Goshen Bridge

World Guide Number: 38-15-7; 38-23-02

Location: At the intersection of Goshen and Boot Roads, connecting Willistown Township, Chester County, Pennsylvania, with Newtown Township, Delaware County, Pennsylvania

Body of Water Crossed: Crum Creek

Length: 80 feet

Width: 18 feet

Year Built: 1860

Built by: Ferdinand Wood

Named for: A neighboring landowner named Mordecai Bartram

Number of Spans: 1

Structural Design: Burr truss arch

Open to Vehicular Traffic: No

National Register Listing: Yes, as part of the 1980 Covered Bridges of Chester County Thematic Resources listing

Description: The bridge's portals display unique slanted planks, while the remainder of its siding is horizontal planks. The portals and siding are dark red in color.

Rehabilitation: Closed to traffic in 1941, the bridge was restored in the mid-1990s. It was further updated and repaired in the mid-2010s.

History: Though it is a display bridge closed to traffic, the Bartram's Covered Bridge is the only intercounty covered bridge connecting Chester County to Delaware County. The bridge is maintained by a joint preservation commission. No other covered bridges remain in Delaware County, once home to more than thirty covered bridges. In 2010, the two surrounding townships celebrated the bridge's 150th birthday and even published a book commemorating the bridge.

Prior to renovations, the Bartram's Covered Bridge displayed a slogan commensurate with its early days: "Lincoln, Save Union and Congress." A marker at the bridge states that the bridge was designed to be "hi and wide as a load of hay," and the costs were split between the counties.

Local/Cultural History: The name "Crum Creek" derives from "crooked creek" in Dutch. Crum Creek begins in a swamp near Newtown Square, Pennsylvania, and flows into the Delaware River.

Bartram's Covered Bridge in May 2015 and February 2022. *Photos courtesy of Jim and Gloria Smedley, ©2015 and 2022*

Gibson's Covered Bridge

Also Known as: County Bridge #120; Harmony Hill Bridge

World Guide Number: 38-15-10

Location: Harmony Hill Road, East and West Bradford Townships, just east of US Route 322

Body of Water Crossed: East Branch of Brandywine Creek

Length: 78 feet

Width: 14 feet

Year Built: Original in 1870; rebuilt in 1872

Built by: Edward H. Hall and Thomas E. Schull

Named for: Local farmer James Gibson

Number of Spans: 1

Structural Design: Burr arch truss

Open to Vehicular Traffic: Yes

National Register Listing: Yes, as part of the 1980 Covered Bridges of Chester County Thematic Resources listing

Description: This bridge has white horizontal planks on its sides and steplike portals. On one side, it has two windows around the king post in the center of the bridge.

Rehabilitation: The original bridge built at this site in 1870 cost $969 to build but was destroyed by flood in 1871. The 1872 replacement bridge cost $2,666. Repairs and improvements in 1959 cost $3,400. Flood damage in 1999 caused the bridge to be closed while repairs were made. It was rehabilitated in 2003. Flood damage from the remnants of Hurricane Ida caused damage to the flooring, siding, and parapets in September 2021. The bridge was closed to traffic for several months while it was repaired but was reopened by early 2022.

History: Gibson's Covered Bridge is the last surviving of the 11 covered bridges that once crossed the East Branch of the Brandywine. A trolley station used to stand near the bridge.

Local/Cultural History: US Route 322 is a historic road that runs from Ohio to New Jersey, connecting the northwestern corner of Pennsylvania with the southeastern corner and passing through the state capital on its way. According to legend, the highway is haunted by Revolutionary War general Anthony Wayne, nicknamed "Mad" Anthony Wayne for his fiery personality. Wayne was from Chester County, residing most of his life at his family's estate, Waynesborough, in Paoli.

Wayne died from complications relating to gout in 1796 on his way home from a western military post. His body was buried at Fort Presque Isle, near Erie, Pennsylvania, but several years later was disinterred to be taken to his family's cemetery plot in Radnor, Pennsylvania. Wayne's son, who called for the body, had underestimated the space the body would require for transportation. He decided to take only the bones and had the body boiled to free the bones of the skin and other elements. The bones were then stuffed into bags and carried to Radnor by the son. The balance of the remains was reinterred in Presque Isle. Not only did Wayne end up spread across two burial places, but legend holds that the son's traveling bags were not secure. Pieces of the body fell out along the road—what is now Route 322—and ever since, the ghost of "Mad" Anthony Wayne walks the road looking for his bones.

Gibson's Covered Bridge in 2015, 2009, and 2022. *Photos courtesy of Jim and Gloria Smedley, ©2009–2022*

Glen Hope Covered Bridge

Also Known as: County Bridge No. 40; Elk Mills

World Guide Number: 38-15-02

Location: Hickory Hill Road, Elk Township, Chester County, Pennsylvania

Body of Water Crossed: Little Elk Creek

Length: 65 feet

Width: 16 feet

Year Built: Original in 1889; reconstructed in 1991

Built by: Menander Wood and George E. Jones

Named for: No explanation found.

Number of Spans: 1

Structural Design: Burr arch truss

Open to Vehicular Traffic: Yes

National Register Listing: Yes, as part of the 1980 Covered Bridges of Chester County Thematic Resources listing

Description: This bridge has white horizontal planks on its portal and dark-stained vertical planks on its sides.

Rehabilitation: After its driver ignored the posted 3-ton weight limit, a 20-ton cement truck fell through the bridge in the 1960s. Steel stringers were added to strengthen the floor of the bridge. Arson destroyed the bridge in 1987, and it was rebuilt in 1990-91.

History: The original bridge was built at a cost of slightly less than $1,800. Glen Hope crosses at what was called Anderson's Ford, after local farmer John Anderson.

Local/Cultural History: Big Elk Creek forms Elk Township's eastern boundary. Hickory Hill and Lewisville are two historic towns in the township. The village of Hickory Hill was formerly known as Nottinghamdale, until 1850. The village of Lewisville sprung up at the meeting point of several roads: Route 472, Route 841, and Strickersville Road. The first post office was established in Lewisville in 1848.

Glen Hope Covered Bridge in 2013 and 2015. *Photos courtesy of Jim and Gloria Smedley, ©2013–2015*

Hall's Covered Bridge

Also Known as: County Bridge #194; Sheeder's Covered Bridge;Sheeder-Hall Covered Bridge; Hall's Sheeder Covered Bridge

World Guide Number: 38-15-12

Location: Hollow Road, East and West Vincent Townships

Body of Water Crossed: Birch Run, where it enters French Creek

Length: 116 feet

Width: 15 feet

Year Built: 1850

Built by: Robert Russell and Jacob Fox

Named for: Two local families named Hall and Sheeder who owned property nearby.

Number of Spans: 1

Structural Design: Burr arch truss

Open to Vehicular Traffic: Yes

National Register Listing: Yes, in 1973. Also mentioned in the 1980 Covered Bridges of Chester County Thematic Resources listing.

Description: This bridge features red clapboard siding that runs horizontally, and stepped portals that are painted white. A pier supports the center of the bridge.

Rehabilitation: The bridge has been reinforced with steel I-beam supports. News articles from 2002 indicate the bridge was damaged by a truck, and the township was not pleased that the Pennsylvania Department of Transportation did not follow historical standards in repairing the bridge.

Repairs were made in 2017 and again in 2018 to fix vehicular damage.

History: Hall's Covered Bridge is the oldest covered bridge in Chester County. Its 1850 construction cost was $1,564.

Local/Cultural History: Originally called Saukanac Creek by the Native Americans, French Creek is a tributary of the Schuylkill River. The creek flows down from French Creek State Park, which straddles Chester County's northwestern border with Berks County, to Phoenixville. Modern Route 23 follows a Native American trail, the French Creek Trail, which ran from the mouth of French Creek in Phoenixville to the Susquehanna River in Columbia, Lancaster County.

Hall's Covered Bridge in 2018 and 2015. *Photos courtesy of Jim and Gloria Smedley, ©2015–2018*

Hayes Clark Covered Bridge

Also Known as: County Bridge #79

World Guide Number: 38-15-07#2

Location: Originally, the bridge was located on Doe Run, near its junction with Buck Run. It later became part of the Buck and Doe Run Farms, a subsidiary of the Texas King Ranch. Today, the bridge is owned by the Brandywine Conservancy and located on private property.

Body of Water Crossed: Doe Run

Length: 75 feet

Width: 16 feet

Year Built: Original in 1884; reconstructed in 1971

Built by: Menander Wood and James Denithorne (original bridge)

Named for: Local farmer and creamery owner Hayes Clark

Number of Spans: 1

Structural Design: Queen post truss

Open to Vehicular Traffic: No

National Register Listing: No

Description: This unpainted bridge has vertical planks on its sides and portal. An unusual feature of this and the Speakman No. 2 bridge is that the wing walls feature stones standing on their ends instead of round or smoothed tops.

Rehabilitation: The bridge was destroyed by a 1963 fire and rebuilt in 1971.

History: The Hayes Clark Covered Bridge is a twin to the Speakman No. 2 Covered Bridge. It cost just over $2,500 when it was originally built. Arthur James's *Covered Bridges of Chester County, Pennsylvania* reports a Clark family story that Hayes Clark told the bridge's builders they had chosen a poor location. It was twice built on the spot he warned against and twice destroyed by floods. Finally, the bridge was rebuilt in 1884 where Mr. Clark suggested, and there it stood until destroyed by fire in 1963.

Local/Cultural History: The Hayes Clark and Speakman No. 2 Covered Bridges were once part of the King Ranch, which owned land in Chester County and across the world. Beginning in 1946, the Chester County property was a successful cattle-grazing area. In the 1980s, more than 5,000 acres of the former King Ranch property were placed under permanent conservation easement, one of the largest in the eastern United States.

The Hayes Clark and its twin bridge are located on private property within the Brandywine Conservancy's Laurel Preserve. Their quiet, off-the-beaten-track setting is idyllic and well worth the visit. For information on how to visit the bridges, contact the Brandywine Conservancy.

Hayes Clark Covered Bridge in 2009 and 2015. *Photos courtesy of Jim and Gloria Smedley, ©2009–2015*

Kennedy Covered Bridge

Also Known as: County Bridge #190

World Guide Number: 38-15-13#2

Location: Seven Stars Road, just north of Kimberton, between East and West Vincent Townships, Chester County, Pennsylvania

Body of Water Crossed: French Creek

Length: 116 feet

Width: 14 feet

Year Built: Original in 1856; rebuilt in 1988

Built by: Jesse King and Alexander Kennedy

Named for: Neighboring landowner Alexander Kennedy

Number of Spans: 1

Structural Design: Burr arch truss

Open to Vehicular Traffic: Yes

National Register Listing: Yes, in 1974. Also mentioned in the 1980 Covered Bridges of Chester County Thematic Resources listing.

Description: Kennedy Bridge has horizontal planks on its dark-stained sides and white portal. The portal is stepped, and the bridge has windows at its midpoint.

Rehabilitation: The original bridge was repaired after flood damage in 1884. Reinforcements were added in 1956 to permit heavier loads. Arsonists destroyed the bridge in 1986. Local citizens rallied to rebuild Kennedy Covered Bridge. It became the first bridge in the United States to be reconstructed using ekki timber, a hardwood from central Africa that is resistant to fire and insects. The rebuilt bridge opened in 1988.

History: The original bridge cost $2,149 to build and was dedicated on July 4, 1856. A covered-bridge society sponsored a 100th-birthday celebration in 1956.

Local/Cultural History: Near the bridge stands the private Kimberton Waldorf School, founded in 1941. It is one of more than a thousand Waldorf schools in more than eighty countries that follow the educational philosophies of Austrian Rudolf Steiner. He established his first school in 1919 at the Waldorf Astoria Cigarette Factory in Stuttgart, Germany, for the employees' children. The curriculum is targeted to various levels of child development and a path of personal spiritual research Steiner called anthroposophy. Three hundred children in grades one through twelve attend the Kimberton Waldorf School. Five other Waldorf Schools exist in Pennsylvania.

Kennedy Covered Bridge in 2015. *Photos courtesy of Jim and Gloria Smedley, ©2015*

Knox Covered Bridge

Also Known as: County Bridge #165; Knox-Valley Forge Dam Bridge

World Guide Number: 38-15-15#2

Location: Yellow Spring Road, Tredyffrin Township, near Valley Forge National Historical Park

Body of Water Crossed: Valley Creek

Length: Original was 50 feet; current bridge is 65 feet

Width: 13 feet

Year Built: Original in 1851; rebuilt in 1865

Built by: Original by Ferdinand Wood; 1865 bridge by Robert Russell

Named for: There is some dispute as to which Knox is the bridge's namesake. General Henry Knox (1750-1806), a Revolutionary War officer who later became the first US secretary of war, had his headquarters nearby in 1777-78. The other potential namesake is Philander Chase Knox (1853-1921), who was a US senator from Pennsylvania, US attorney general, and US secretary of state. He owned land nearby and is interred in Washington Memorial Cemetery in Valley Forge, Pennsylvania.

Number of Spans: 1

Structural Design: Burr arch truss

Open to Vehicular Traffic: Yes

National Register Listing: Yes, in 1966, as part of Valley Forge National Historic Park

Description: This bridge looks the most "open." Its white siding runs horizontally and is broken by large, open windows at midwall height that run the full length of the bridge. The siding also stops short of the roofline for further ventilation.

Rehabilitation: The current bridge was built in 1865, after a flood that year washed away the original. In 1960, the bridge was strengthened with steel girders. Nearly $200,000 worth of repairs were performed in the mid-1990s. Further rehabilitation was done in 2016.

History: The original Knox Covered Bridge cost $843 to build in 1851; its replacement cost $1,179 in 1865. Local police saved the bridge from fire in 1958. A trailer hauling a load of steel estimated to exceed 30 tons damaged the bridge, which had a posted 15-ton limit, in 1967.

Local/Cultural History: Located within proximity to Valley Forge National Historical Park, Knox Covered Bridge is reputed to be the most photographed covered bridge in Chester County. Many who visit the bridge fail to realize that it came decades after the American troops under General George Washington established their winter encampment here in 1777. Most stories about the Valley Forge quarters paint a grim picture. The National Park Service's website states that this romanticized story about the encampment was intended to teach Americans a lesson about perseverance. While there were hardships at Valley Forge, the soldiers had supplies and built approximately two thousand small, wooden huts for accommodations. Most of the men who died at Valley Forge were stricken by disease in the early spring months.

Knox Covered Bridge in 2015. *Photo courtesy of Jim and Gloria Smedley, ©2015*

Larkin's Mill Covered Bridge

Also Known as: Dorlan's Mill Bridge; County Bridge #128

World Guide Number: 38-15-11#2

Location: Originally, on Milford Road. Today, in Byers Station (residential development), at the intersection of Byers Station and Graphite Mine Roads, Upper Uwchlan Township, Chester County, Pennsylvania

Body of Water Crossed: Originally, Marsh Creek; currently, a small unnamed stream

Length: 60 feet

Width: 14.5 feet

Year Built: Original in 1854; rebuilt in 1881; relocated in 1972; rehabilitated and moved to current location in 2006

Built by: Menander and Ferdinand Wood in 1881

Named for: Jesse Larkin, who owned a mill near the bridge's original location

Number of Spans: 1

Structural Design: Burr arch truss

Open to Vehicular Traffic: No

National Register Listing: Yes, as part of the 1980 Covered Bridges of Chester County Thematic Resources listing

Description: The bridge has vertical-siding planks that appear to be unstained. It has no windows, but the siding stops short of the roofline, allowing for ventilation. The bridge sits on concrete abutments and lacks parapets.

Rehabilitation: The Larkin's Mill Covered Bridge was rebuilt in 1881 for $893. It was rehabilitated and relocated in 2006.

History: When the State of Pennsylvania decided to flood Marsh Creek to form a reservoir, Upper Uwchlan Township insisted that the state save Larkin's Mill Covered Bridge. Had it not been moved, the bridge would be covered by approximately 60 feet of water of the 535-acre lake. The bridge was moved in 1970 to another area of what became the Marsh Creek State Park. It cost more than $19,000 to move the bridge. The bridge sat neglected in a field for more than 30 years. In the 1990s, the township purchased the bridge from the state for $1. Beginning in 2005, a collective effort of the township and builders restored the bridge. The bridge was disassembled at the park, restored by a timber company in Bucks County, Pennsylvania, and returned to its new home within a development on Upper Uwchlan Township's trail system. The process included replacing some of the bridge's timber with white oak, while attempting to retain as much of the 1854 materials as possible. The rehabilitated bridge reopened in the spring of 2006 with an official ceremony that also celebrated the township's 150th anniversary. The rehabilitation was funded primarily by developers and a small state grant.

Local/Cultural History: Larkin's Mill Covered Bridge is located near the village of Eagle. A tavern has existed at the fork of the two main roads that cross here (including what is now Route 100) since the early 1700s (though its building is of a later date). The Eagle Tavern inspired the growth of the surrounding town, of which several historic structures remain. Today the surrounding community reflects the vast changes in the Chester County landscape over the past four decades. Once the setting of farmland and rural mill towns, the suburban area now exhibits high-density housing and commercial development.

Larkin's Mill Covered Bridge in 2015. *Photos courtesy of Jim and Gloria Smedley, ©2015*

Linton Stevens Covered Bridge

Also Known as: County Bridge # 28; Linton Stephens

World Guide Number: 38-15-03

Location: Kings Row Road, Elk Township, Chester County, Pennsylvania

Body of Water Crossed: Big Elk Creek

Length: 102 feet

Width: 15 feet

Year Built: Original in 1875; rebuilt in 1884

Built by: J. Denithorne and son

Named for: Linton Stevens (Stephens), who was the postmaster and general-store owner in nearby Hickory Hill

Number of Spans: 1

Structural Design: Burr arch truss

Open to Vehicular Traffic: Yes

National Register Listing: Yes, as part of the 1980 Covered Bridges of Chester County, Thematic Resources listing

Description: The bridge has white horizontal planks on its portal and dark-stained vertical planks on its sides.

Rehabilitation: The bridge was closed in the mid-1990s for rehabilitation and reopened in 1996. The bridge has been reinforced with steel I-beam supports.

History: An iron bridge was built at this site in 1875 but was replaced with the covered bridge after destruction by the 1884 flood.

Local/Cultural History: The Linton Stevens Covered Bridge stands virtually at the boundary meeting point of East Nottingham, New London, and Elk Townships. Elk Township was carved out of East Nottingham Township in 1857.

Linton Stevens Covered Bridge in 2015. *Photos courtesy of Jim and Gloria Smedley, ©2015*

Mercer's Mill Covered Bridge

Also Known as: Mercer's Ford Covered Bridge; County Bridge #10

World Guide Number: 38-15-19; 38-36-38

Location: Bailey's Crossroads, connecting West Fallowfield Township in Chester County, Pennsylvania, with Sadsbury Township in Lancaster County, Pennsylvania

Body of Water Crossed: East Branch of Octoraro Creek

Length: 103 feet

Width: 15 feet

Year Built: 1880

Built by: J. Brinton Carter

Named for: Local farmer and mill owner Captain John Mercer

Number of Spans: 1

Structural Design: Burr arch truss

Open to Vehicular Traffic: Yes

National Register Listing: Yes, as part of the 1980 Covered Bridges of Lancaster County Thematic Resource listing

Description: The bridge's siding is of red vertical planks, except for the portals, where the white planks run horizontally. The bridge has a window on one side at the Creek Road end. The parapets extend into the bridge, where they are capped with wood.

Rehabilitation: The bridge received painting and new siding in 1991, and additional repairs in 1996. It has been well kept since then.

History: The bridge cost almost $1,700 to build in 1880, with each county paying half. The Mercer's Mill Covered Bridge survived (undamaged) an arson attempt in November 2005.

In his *Covered Bridges of Chester County, Pennsylvania*, Arthur James noted that Congressman Paul B. Dague, who represented Chester and Lancaster Counties from 1948 to 1968, displayed a framed color photograph of Mercer's Mill Covered Bridge in his office.

Local/Cultural History: The name "Octoraro," also spelled as "Octorara," is derived from a Native American word for "running water."

Rising in the town of Christiana, Lancaster County, Pennsylvania, the East Branch of Octoraro Creek forms the southern boundary between Lancaster and Chester Counties and flows under the Mercer's Mill Covered Bridge. The West Branch of Octoraro Creek flows through Lancaster County under the Jackson's Mill and White Rock Forge Covered Bridges. South of the meeting point of the two branches, the creek is dammed to form Octoraro Lake. From there, the main branch flows under the Pine Grove Covered Bridge and down into Maryland on its way to the Susquehanna River.

Mercer's Mill Covered Bridge in 2015 and 2013. *Photos courtesy of Jim and Gloria Smedley, ©2013–2015*

Pine Grove Covered Bridge

Also Known as: County Bridge #7

World Guide Number: 38-15-22#3; 38-36-41#3

Location: Connects Forge Road in Lower Oxford Township, Chester County, Pennsylvania, with Ashville Road in Little Britain Township, Lancaster County, Pennsylvania

Body of Water Crossed: Octoraro Creek, south of the Octoraro Reservoir

Length: 204 feet

Width: 15 feet

Year Built: Original in 1816; rebuilt in 1846 and 1884

Built by: Joseph Elliot and Robert Russell in 1846; rebuilt in 1884 by Elias McMellen, who served as a captain in the Civil War. McMellen began building bridges in 1859 and had built more than 20 covered bridges by 1884.

Named for: Nearby pine-filled woods

Number of Spans: 2

Structural Design: Burr arch truss

Open to Vehicular Traffic: Yes

National Register Listing: Yes, as part of the 1980 Covered Bridges of Lancaster County Thematic Resources. The Thematic Resource listing described Pine Grove as "one of the longest covered bridges in the state" and noted, "The two Burr arch spans do slightly bow."

Description: Pine Grove is the only two-span covered bridge in Chester County. It bears red-painted vertical siding and white vertical planks on its portals. The bridge has windows on either side where the center support divides the two arches. Long parapets line the portal on both sides.

Rehabilitation: In 2007-08, the bridge was refurbished by J. D. Eckman, Inc., for the Pennsylvania Department of Transportation. The bridge was taken off its piers. The abutments and piers were rebuilt in concrete. Some of the wood paneling was replaced with sturdy wood from the Pacific Northwest. Steel beams were added to support the bridge and improve its load-carrying capacity. The $3.7 million rehabilitation project concluded in August 2008, when the bridge reopened to traffic. An oversized truck caused minor damage to some overhead beams in March 2010.

History: The current Pine Grove Bridge is the third on its site since 1816, when the bridge was the first to connect Chester and Lancaster Counties. Initially, the bridge was important to facilitate stagecoach traffic on the national highway from New York City to Washington, DC. After a storm destroyed the original bridge, it was replaced in 1846 at a cost of almost $1,500. Ice destroyed the second bridge. Construction of the 1884 replacement cost $4,450.

The bridge is owned by the Commonwealth of Pennsylvania.

Local/Cultural History: Around 1950, the Chester Municipal Authority (now the Chester Water Authority) purchased the water rights to Octoraro Creek. The authority built a large dam and pumping station to transport water to the city of Chester, 40 miles away. The project included creation of Octoraro Reservoir, which flooded the locations of two other covered bridges in the Oxford area.

Near the dam at Pine Grove stands a small stone pump house, built around 1904. In 1953, local artist Charles X. Carlson, a founding member and leader of the Octoraro Art Association, inquired about using the building as a meeting place and studio. The water company and the art association struck a deal that took effect in 1954: the art association could use the building as a studio and meeting place for the payment of one painting a year. As a result, the OAA held a contest each September to select the Picture of the Year from its members' work. In 2009, they selected a "People's Choice" winner that was a painting by Ruth Lefever of the Pine Grove Covered Bridge.

Pine Grove Covered Bridge in 2015 and 2009. *Photos courtesy of Jim and Gloria Smedley, ©2009–2015*

Rapps Dam Covered Bridge

Also Known as: Rapps Covered Bridge; County Bridge #188

World Guide Number: 38-15-14

Location: Rapps Dam Road, East Pikeland Township

Body of Water Crossed: French Creek

Length: 122 feet

Width: 14 feet

Year Built: 1866

Built by: Benjamin F. Hartman

Named for: George A. Rapp, a Civil War veteran who owned a mill nearby; Rapp was also the maiden name of builder Benjamin Hartman's wife

Number of Spans: 1

Structural Design: Burr arch truss

Open to Vehicular Traffic: Yes

National Register Listing: Yes, in 1973. Also mentioned in the 1980 Covered Bridges of Chester County Thematic Resources listing.

Description: The horizontal siding planks of this bridge are stained dark. The portals have white horizontal planks and boxed cornices with an ornate decoration. Windows on each side run most of the length of the bridge.

Rehabilitation: The bridge was repaired at a cost of approximately $7,000 after Hurricane Agnes caused substantial damage in 1972. The sign on the bridge's portal states that the Pennsylvania Department of Transportation rehabilitated the bridge in 1977.

The bridge has been rehabilitated several times to address damage from oversized vehicles and flooding. The bridge was reopened in 2011, following a $1.5 million rehabilitation that entailed replacing the cedar shake roof, redwood siding, and wood decking, as well as several steel support beams. The abutments and wing walls were also repaired. Prior to its closure for that project, more than 4,300 vehicles per day crossed the bridge.

Additional repairs were made in 2015 for damage from vehicles and flooding. The bridge was already closed for repairs from vehicle damage when the remnants of Hurricane Ida swept through in September 2021, causing additional damage. The bridge was open to traffic by January 2022.

History: The Rapps Dam Covered Bridge cost $3,595 to build in 1866.

Local/Cultural History: Rapps Dam Covered Bridge is located not far from the Kimberton Village Historic District in East Pikeland Township. The township is named for Irishman Joseph Pike, who was granted 10,000 acres in Chester County by William Penn in 1705. Pike's land was established as Pikeland Township in 1745 and divided into East Pikeland and West Pikeland in 1838.

Rapps Dam Covered Bridge in 2015. *Photos courtesy of Jim and Gloria Smedley, ©2015*

Rudolph and Arthur Covered Bridge

Also Known as: County Bridge #26

World Guide Number: 38-15-01

Location: Camp Bonsul Road between Elk and New London Townships, Chester County, Pennsylvania

Body of Water Crossed: Big Elk Creek

Length: 90 feet

Width: 15 feet

Year Built: 1880 [destroyed by remnants of Hurricane Ida on September 1, 2021]

Built by: Menander Wood and Richard T. Meredith

Named for: Local paper-mill owners named Rudolph and Arthur

Number of Spans: 1

Structural Design: Burr arch truss

National Register Listing: Yes, as part of the 1980 Covered Bridges of Chester County Thematic Resources listing

Description: This bridge had vertical planks painted white on the exterior of its sides and portal.

Rehabilitation: The original 1880 bridge was repaired after flood damage in 1884 at a cost of almost $800 and in 1915 at a cost of almost $1,400. It was also repaired after floods in 1999. Sadly, the bridge washed away due to the remnants of Hurricane Ida in September 2021. The Commonwealth of Pennsylvania intends to replace the bridge, most likely with a covered bridge.

History: Construction of the original bridge cost slightly more than $2,300.

Local/Cultural History: Big Elk Creek rises in east and west branches near Cochranville, while Little Elk Creek rises southeast of Oxford. Big Elk and Little Elk Creeks meet in Elkton, Maryland, to form the Elk River, which flows into the Chesapeake Bay.

Rudolph and Arthur's Covered Bridge in 2015. *Photos courtesy of Jim and Gloria Smedley, ©2015*

Speakman No. 1 Covered Bridge

Also Known as: County Bridge #74

World Guide Number: 38-15-05

Location: Frog Hollow Road, connecting East Fallowfield and West Marlborough Townships, north of Doe Run

Body of Water Crossed: Buck Run Creek

Length: 75 feet

Width: 14 feet

Year Built: 1881

Built by: Menander and Ferdinand Wood

Named for: Local gristmill owner Jonathan Speakman

Number of Spans: 1

Structural Design: Burr arch truss

Open to Vehicular Traffic: Yes

National Register Listing: Yes, as part of the 1980 Covered Bridges of Chester County Thematic Resources listing

Description: The bridge has vertical planks on the siding and portal. The siding is red, while the portals are a dark stain.

Rehabilitation: The bridge survived a fire in 1959, with little damage. The bridge was repaired after an incident in 2011, when a tractor trailer damaged the bridge. A local resident heard the impact, called 911, and followed the truck until police could pull it over. The bridge was closed in 2011 for a $1.9 million rehabilitation, which included the addition of steel support beams, and was reopened in 2016.

History: The Speakman No. 1 Covered Bridge cost $1,938 to build. It is surrounded by an area known for cattle grazing and fox hunting.

Local/Cultural History: The bridge is just north of the village of Doe Run. The Doe Run Village Historic District is listed on the National Register of Historic Places. The district covers more than 500 acres, including the viewshed of this sprawling village. Among the features of the historic district is the stone gristmill built by William Harlan in 1744. It had a working waterwheel until 1937. Driving through the village today, motorists will see a "Blow horn" sign painted on the side of the mill at the intersection of Doe Run and Springdell Roads.

Beginning in 1919, the village and much of its surrounding lands were purchased by Lammot DuPont as part of a plan to create a reservoir to protect the high-quality water in the Doe Run watershed. In 1946, the King Ranch of Texas purchased DuPont's almost 8,000 acres in the area and operated a large-scale cattle-grazing operation there for several decades. More than 5,000 acres of the King Ranch were placed under a conservation easement in 1984.

Speakman No. 1 Covered Bridge in 2016. *Photos courtesy of Jim and Gloria Smedley, ©2016*

Speakman No. 2 Covered Bridge

Also Known as: Mary Ann Pyle Covered Bridge; County Bridge #73

World Guide Number: 38-15-06

Location: Originally, the bridge was located over Buck Run after traveling over the Hayes Clark Covered Bridge. Today, the bridge is owned by the Brandywine Conservancy and located on private property.

Body of Water Crossed: Buck Run Creek

Length: 75 feet

Width: 15 feet

Year Built: 1881

Built by: Menander and Ferdinand Wood

Named for: Mary Ann Pyle, the daughter of a local landowner, James B. Pyle

Number of Spans: 1

Structural Design: Queen post truss

Open to Vehicular Traffic: No

National Register Listing: Yes, as part of the 1980 Covered Bridges of Chester County Thematic Resources listing

Description: The bridge has vertical planks on its red sides and white portal. Like the Hayes Clark Bridge, the Speakman No. 2 Covered Bridge has stones placed on end in its wing walls.

Rehabilitation: Arthur James's *Covered Bridges of Chester County, Pennsylvania* indicates that two previous bridges stood on the site of this bridge and were destroyed by floods. In 2005-2006, new siding and steel support beams were added to the Speakman No. 2 / Mary Ann Pyle Covered Bridge. The bridge was rehabilitated in 2016.

History: The Speakman No. 2 / Mary Ann Pyle Covered Bridge is a twin to the Hayes Clark Covered Bridge. Its original construction cost was $2,000.

Local/Cultural History: The Speakman No. 2 Covered Bridge and its twin once stood a quarter mile apart and now are located (still near each other) on private property within the Brandywine Conservancy's Laurel Preserve. Their quiet, off-the-beaten-track setting is idyllic and well worth the visit. For information on how to visit the bridges, contact the Brandywine Conservancy.

Speakman No. 2 Covered Bridge in 2015. *Photos courtesy of Jim and Gloria Smedley, ©2015*

Stringers in the White Clay Creek Preserve

Location: Two covered stringers stand within the White Clay Creek Preserve in Landenberg, Pennsylvania.

The longer stringer is at the entrance to the Penn-Del Trail from Parking Lot #1 on London Tract Road, just south of where London Tract splits off from Broad Run Road at the Y with Good Hope Road.

The other stringer bends across the beams of an old crossing. From the preserve entrance on Arc Corner Road, follow the trail southeast to the bridge.

Body of Water Crossed: White Clay Creek

Local/Cultural History: Beginning in the 1950s, the DuPont Company in Delaware began purchasing land along White Clay Creek, with the goal of damming the creek to create a reservoir that would supply the water needs of the company and growing New Castle County, Delaware. But DuPont encountered a strong grassroots resistance that ultimately led to the company abandoning its plans and donating the land to form a bistate preserve in 1984. Since then, both states have added to the preserved land, and White Clay Creek has been designated a federal Wild and Scenic River. Today, the White Clay Creek Preserve in Pennsylvania covers more than 1,300 acres, while the White Clay State Park in Delaware has 4,000 acres.

Abundant in natural resources, the park is also rich in history. The London Tract Meeting House, at the corner of Sharpless and London Tract Roads in Pennsylvania, dates to 1729. Until destroyed by arsonists in 1960, the Yeatman Covered Bridge stood nearby on Sharpless Road, past the Yeatman Mansion. Within the parks stand several boundary markers surveyed and set by Charles Mason and Jeremiah Dixon in the 1760s.

TWO NEARBY COVERED BRIDGES ON THE OCTORARO, LANCASTER COUNTY, PENNSYLVANIA

Jackson's Mill Covered Bridge

Also Known as: Jackson's Mill Eichelbergers Store; West Octoraro Bridge No. 1

World Guide Number: 38-36-33#2

Location: Mt. Pleasant Road, near its intersection with Hollow Road, Bart Township, Lancaster County, Pennsylvania

Body of Water Crossed: West Branch of Octoraro Creek

Length: 143 feet

Width: 15 feet

Year Built: Original in 1878; rebuilt in 1985

Built by: Samuel Stauffer in 1878; Lancaster County and Stephen Esh in 1985

Named for: David W. Jackson's Mill

Number of Spans: 1

Structural Design: Burr arch truss

Open to Vehicular Traffic: Yes

National Register Listing: No. It was previously registered as part of the Covered Bridges of Lancaster County Thematic Resources but removed in 1986.

Description: This bridge features vertical-siding planks that are red on the interior and exterior, and white horizontal planks on the portal. It has a window on one side at the opening on the south end, near the intersection of Mt. Pleasant and Hollow Roads, and windows on each side at the bridge's midpoint behind the king post. Only one of the four wing walls extends up into a parapet at the bridge's opening. The original bridge was placed "on a skew," or at a slant, rather than perpendicular, across the creek.

Rehabilitation: The original bridge cost $2,500. The bridge was washed off its foundation in a 1985 flood and rebuilt at a higher level at a cost of $75,000. A sign painted inside the bridge says it was "rehabbed" in 2005.

History: One of my earliest memories of covered bridges is of Jackson's Mill. When I was eight years old, my father took a detour on our way home from my grandparents' house on a Sunday afternoon to see the bridge after the 1985 flood. I remember seeing the bridge resting in shambles on the opposite shore, like a barn that had been uprooted and dropped on the banks of the creek. I barely recognized the site when I returned twenty years later to photograph the bridge. It's a quiet, serene setting surrounded by woods and an Amish farm. There is a lovely view of the bridge in the valley from the hill on Mt. Pleasant Road.

Local/Cultural History: Bart Township is the home of this bridge. The township's name derives from the abbreviation "Bart.," for Baronet.

A large portion of the population in Bart Township is Amish. The Amish are Anabaptist Christians who choose to live plain lives separate from the non-Amish world and without modern conveniences, such as cars and electricity. The name "Amish" comes from Jakob Amman, who led a split from a Swiss sect in the 1690s. The Amish immigrated to America in the eighteenth century. Today, Amish people live in more than thirty US states, mostly in rural communities, and typically work as farmers, as carpenters, or in related trades. Pennsylvania is home to the largest population of Amish, at approximately 87,000, of which about 40,000 live in Lancaster County.

Jackson's Mill Covered Bridge in 2013, 2019, and 2015. *Photos courtesy of Jim and Gloria Smedley, ©2013–2019*

White Rock Forge Covered Bridge

Also Known as: White Rock Covered Bridge; West Octoraro Bridge No. 2

World Guide Number: 38-36-18#2

Location: White Rock Road, connecting Little Britain and Colerain Townships, Kirkwood, Lancaster County, Pennsylvania

Body of Water Crossed: West Branch of Octoraro Creek

Length: 113 feet

Width: 15 feet

Year Built: Original in 1847; rebuilt in 1884

Built by: John Russell in 1847; Elias McMellen in 1884

Named for: The nearby White Rock Forge (no longer existing)

Number of Spans: 1

Structural Design: Burr arch truss

Open to Vehicular Traffic: Yes

National Register Listing: Yes, as part of the 1980 Covered Bridges of Lancaster County Thematic Resources listing

Description: The bridge has red siding, inside and out, and white portals. The siding runs vertically and has windows on each side at the south end of the bridge.

Rehabilitation: The bridge was destroyed and rebuilt in 1884.

History: This is the second-oldest covered bridge still open to traffic in Lancaster County.

Local/Cultural History: The White Rock Forge Covered Bridge is a busy place every February 2. The members of the adjacent Slumbering Groundhog Lodge gather here each year to celebrate Groundhog Day. Their white nightshirts and black top hats stand out against the red covered bridge they gather in front of to begin their annual parade. The procession leads to the Pinnacle of Prognostication (a manure spreader decorated for the occasion). After opening ceremonies, skits, and announcement of whether the prognosticating groundhog Octoraro Orphie saw his shadow, the members gather by the side of Octoraro Creek to initiate a class of new members by dunking one in the chilly waters. Founded in 1908, the lodge has more than two hundred members. The Groundhog Day ceremonies are open to the public.

White Rock Covered Bridge in 2009, 2013, and 2020. *Photos courtesy of Jim and Gloria Smedley, ©2009–2020*

COVERED BRIDGES OF CECIL COUNTY, MARYLAND

Gilpin's Falls Covered Bridge

Also Known as: Gilpin's Covered Bridge; Gilpin Falls Covered Bridge

World Guide Number: 20-07-01

Location: Along Route 272 in Bay View, Cecil County, Maryland

Body of Water Crossed: North East Creek

Length: 119 feet

Width: 13.5 feet

Year Built: Circa 1850 to 1860

Built by: George Johnson

Named for: Samuel Gilpin, a nearby mill owner

Number of Spans: 1

Structural Design: Burr arch truss

Open to Vehicular Traffic: No

National Register Listing: Yes, as of December 3, 2008

Description: The bridge features windows in the middle of the span and wall boards that stop short of the roof, permitting ventilation and light through the bridge. It also exhibits two arches, one above the other.

Rehabilitation: A significant rehabilitation of Gilpin's Falls Covered Bridge began in early 2009. Though it had stood for 150 years, the bridge was severely deteriorated and on the verge of collapse.

The bridge was stripped down to its frame, revealing the truss arch supports to passersby along Route 272. Most of the original white-pine arches were saved, but some end pieces had to be replaced. With an effort toward matching the replacements to the original type, the rehabilitation used five different woods for the framing, decking, siding, rafters, and sections near the water.

The rehabilitation did not involve moving the bridge; rather, steel beams were placed next to the bridge and used to create a platform, from which the crew could work on the bridge in its original location. The project was completed in 2010.

History: Gilpin's Falls Covered Bridge cost approximately $2,000 to build in 1860. When State Route 272 was built in the 1930s, the bridge was bypassed. A big snowstorm in 1958 destroyed the roof, which was repaired in 1959. At that time, the bridge was owned by the State of Maryland.

In the 1980s, a town on the Eastern Shore of Maryland sought to obtain the bridge. But locals of Cecil County formed a committee that advocated to keep the bridge in its original location. The lobbying efforts of the Gilpin's Falls Covered Bridge Committee resulted in the state giving the bridge to Cecil County, along with $50,000 for maintenance. The committee maintained the bridge for years, cutting brush and cleaning up trash. In 1989, the committee and county repaired the bridge's roof, siding, and wing walls. Eventually, however, the bridge deteriorated to a point that required closing it even to pedestrian traffic in the 1990s, and a substantial rehabilitation was necessary to preserve the bridge.

After years of lobbying, securing the bridge's designation as a Cecil County Historic Trust Property, and listing on the National Register of Historic Places, the committee finally got the support of the county for the rehabilitation. The project cost approximately $1.4 million. The cost was paid from federal and county funds, the original grant of maintenance money from the state (which had nearly doubled from the accumulation of interest over twenty years), and more than $29,000 raised by the committee from donations.

Local/Cultural History: Only six covered bridges stand in Maryland. The Gilpin's Falls and Foxcatcher Farm Covered Bridges are the last remaining covered bridges in Cecil County. Gilpin's Falls is the longest covered bridge in the state.

The waterway of Gilpin's Falls and its covered bridge were important factors in the local economy of Cecil County. Near the bridge are waterfalls that drop 106 feet over a distance of 2,000 feet. The earliest known mill to harness power from the waterfalls was established by Samuel Gilpin in 1735. Over the years, the site has been used by flour mills, woolen mills, and sawmills.

Farmers used the covered bridge to bring their grain to the mills. Even after the bridge was closed to traffic, some farmers would pull a load under the bridge for cover from the elements. A holding pond and the ruins of several mills and millraces remain near the bridge and are listed on the National Register of Historic Places as the Gilpin's Falls Historic District.

Gilpin's Falls Covered Bridge in 2009, before rehabilitation, and in 2010, after rehabilitation. *Photos courtesy of Jim and Gloria Smedley, ©2009–2010*

Foxcatcher Farm Covered Bridge

Also Known as: Fox Catcher or Foxcatcher's Covered Bridge

World Guide Number: 20-07-02

Location: Tawes Drive, inside the Fair Hill Natural Resource Management Area, Fair Hill, Cecil County, Maryland

Body of Water Crossed: Big Elk Creek

Length: 80 feet

Width: 12 feet

Year Built: 1860

Built by: Ferdinand Wood

Named for: The fox-chasing sport pursued on the land around the bridge while owned by William DuPont Jr.

Number of Spans: 1

Structural Design: Burr arch truss

Open to Vehicular Traffic: No

National Register Listing: No. Maryland designated the bridge a State Historic Civil Engineering Landmark in 1994.

Description: This bridge has red vertical planks on its siding and portals.

Rehabilitation: The bridge was rehabilitated in 1992 and repaired after flood damage in 1999.

History: The bridge was built at the request of the Cecil County Commissioners in 1860 and cost $1,165. Today, Foxcatcher Farm Covered Bridge is one of only two covered bridges remaining in Cecil County, and six in the state of Maryland.

Local/Cultural History: The Foxcatcher Farm Covered Bridge is located on the former estate of William DuPont Jr., who purchased the land in 1927 to enjoy his equestrian and fox-chasing pastimes. In 1975, the State of Maryland purchased the estate, and it became the Fair Hill Natural Resource Management Area. Today, the NRMA consists of more than 5,600 acres and offers trails for biking, hiking, and equestrian riding. Portions of the property are also used to host the Fair Hill Races and the Cecil County Fair. There is no fee to drive through the NRMA; information about fees to park and utilize facilities is available in each parking lot or online.

The NRMA is also the site of the training center that produced the famed horse Barbaro. In May 2006, the thoroughbred won the Kentucky Derby and was a favorite to win the Triple Crown. But an injury during the Preakness left him struggling for his life. Legions of fans rooted for Barbaro while veterinarians at New Bolton Center in Kennett Square, Pennsylvania, spent eight months performing surgeries and other treatments to save the horse. Ultimately, complications from the injury proved too great, and Barbara was euthanized in January 2007.

Visit the Maryland Department of Natural Resources website for more information, maps, and visitor rules relating to the Fair Hill Natural Resource Management Area. Learn more about the county's agricultural heritage at the Cecil County Fair, held in late July each year since 1954.

Foxcatcher Farm Covered Bridge in 2013, 2018, and 2010. *Photos courtesy of Jim and Gloria Smedley, ©2010–2018*

COVERED BRIDGES OF NEW CASTLE COUNTY, DELAWARE

Kayakers cross under Smith's Covered Bridge. *Photo courtesy of Jim and Gloria Smedley, ©2013*

Ashland Covered Bridge

Also Known as: No other name found

World Guide Number: 08-02-02

Location: Barley Mill Road, Ashland, New Castle County, Delaware

Body of Water Crossed: Red Clay Creek

Length: 54 feet

Width: 15 feet

Year Built: Between 1850 and 1865

Built by: Unknown, but possibly by the same person who built Wooddale, which is of a similar construction

Named for: Its location in the community of Ashland

Number of Spans: 1

Structural Design: Town lattice truss

Open to Vehicular Traffic: Yes

National Register Listing: Yes, in 1973

Description: The bridge is painted red on the exterior and white on the interior. Ashland Covered Bridge is called a plank-pin bridge because its planks are secured with pins of hardwood.

Rehabilitation: The deck of Ashland Covered Bridge was rehabilitated in 1964. The bridge underwent rehabilitation in 1982, when steel supports were added. The bridge was again rehabilitated in 2007-2008 at a cost of nearly $435,000. To avoid interference with the migration season of the bog turtle, an endangered species, the project was conducted in two phases and included repairs to the bridge's abutment foundation, wooden substructure, roof, deck, and siding. African bongossi hardwood was used to improve the bridge's resiliency. Less than six months after the bridge reopened in 2008, a vehicle exceeding the portal's size of 12 feet, 3 inches tried to pass through the bridge and damaged the roof, requiring emergency repairs estimated at a cost of $2,000.

History: Delaware was once home to more than a hundred covered bridges. Of the three that stand today, Ashland has the most original elements. Smith's Bridge and Wooddale were destroyed and rebuilt.

Local/Cultural History: Ashland Covered Bridge is adjacent to the Ashland Nature Center, the headquarters for the Delaware Nature Society. Founded in 1964, the organization focuses on environmental education, conservation, preservation, and advocacy and has aided in the preservation of more than 100,000 acres of farmland and open space. DNS was one partner in the effort that succeeded in having the State of Delaware designate the Red Clay Valley Scenic Byway, which recognizes the scenic, natural, and historic resources along a network of twenty-eight rural roads within the Red Clay Watershed in New Castle County. Both Ashland and Wooddale Covered Bridges are within the byway.

Ashland Covered Bridge in 2013. *Photo courtesy of Jim and Gloria Smedley, ©2013*

Smith's Bridge Covered Bridge

Also Known as: Smith's Bridge

World Guide Number: 08-02-01#2

Location: Smith Bridge Road, New Castle County, Delaware

Body of Water Crossed: Brandywine Creek

Length: 154 feet

Width: 15 feet

Year Built: Original in 1839; reconstructed in 2002

Built by: Eastern States Construction Services, Inc.

Named for: Smith's Mill, which stood nearby

Number of Spans: 1

Structural Design: Burr truss arch

Open to Vehicular Traffic: Yes

National Register Listing: No

Description: This red bridge has horizontal planks on its sides and portals, and windows that run most of the length of the bridge.

Rehabilitation: After arsonists destroyed the bridge in 1961, it was replaced with an uncovered structure. Four decades later, working with a community group, the State of Delaware rebuilt the covered bridge, using African bongossi timber, a hardwood that is resistant to rot and fire. Reconstruction cost $1.2 million and included realigning the approaching roadway to improve visibility. Construction began in late July 2002, and the new covered bridge opened with a ceremony on January 11, 2003. An oversized vehicle caused damage to the portal in April 2021, but the bridge remained open and even survived severe flooding (nearly to its roofline) from remnants of Hurricane Ida in September 2021.

History: The original bridge cost just under $5,500. The Smith family owned a mill next to the bridge until 1858, when it was sold to the Twaddels. The mill became known as Twaddel's Mill, but the Smith name continued to be used in reference to the bridge and road. The mill operated until about 1900.

Local/Cultural History: The Brandywine River, or creek as it's called in some locations, runs from southeastern Pennsylvania into Delaware, where it joins the Christina River and flows into the Delaware Bay. The river's name may come from an earlier settler's name or from a legend in which a Dutch ship carrying a spirit named brandy wine wrecked at the stream's mouth.

The Brandywine has played a significant role in the history of the area. It was an important resource to Native Americans. In 1777, the largest land battle of the Revolutionary War took place near the Brandywine in Chadds Ford. Harnessing the waterpower, mills rose along the Brandywine, including paper mills and the gunpowder mills of E. I. DuPont de Nemours. The natural and scenic beauty of the Brandywine valley inspired illustrators Howard Pyle and N. C. Wyeth, as well as N. C.'s son Andrew Wyeth and grandson Jamie Wyeth, whose works can be seen at the Delaware Art Museum in Wilmington, Delaware, and the Brandywine River Museum in Chadds Ford, Pennsylvania.

Smith's Covered Bridge in 2013 and 2003. *Photos courtesy of Jim and Gloria Smedley, ©2003–2013*

Wooddale Covered Bridge

Also Known as: No other names found

World Guide Number: 08-02-04#2

Location: Rolling Mill Road, New Castle County, Delaware

Body of Water Crossed: Red Clay Creek

Length: 60 feet

Width: 16 feet

Year Built: Original circa 1850; rebuilt in 2008

Built by: On the basis of similarity in the bridges, the original Wooddale Covered Bridge may have been built by the same person who built Ashland Covered Bridge. Mumford & Miller Concrete Inc. reconstructed the bridge in 2008.

Named for: Neighboring Wooddale community, which took its name from the Wood family that once owned the nearby mill

Number of Spans: 1

Structural Design: Town lattice truss

Open to Vehicular Traffic: Yes

National Register Listing: Yes, in 1973 (nominated with Ashland Covered Bridge) and in 1979 as part of the Wooddale Historic District

Description: The bridge's exterior is painted red with white trim, while the interior is unpainted.

Rehabilitation: Wooddale covered bridge was washed away by floods from Tropical Storm Henri in September 2003. A temporary bridge crossed the creek for several years until the bridge was reconstructed. The State of Delaware rebuilt Wooddale Covered Bridge, using African bongossi wood and cedar shingles. Construction began in September 2007, and the bridge opened in December 2008. The new bridge cost $3.374 million and is a replica of the original, with a few modifications. The reconstructed bridge was realigned to accommodate larger vehicles and stands an additional 5 feet higher above the creek to provide greater accommodation of floodwater.

History: The original Wooddale Covered Bridge provided access to the Delaware Iron Works. Mills first harnessed the creek's waterpower around 1814 for ironworks, but by the end of the nineteenth century the mills had transformed to paper production.

Local/Cultural History: The Wooddale Covered Bridge serves as the sole access to the residents of the Wooddale community near Centerville, Delaware.

The Wilmington and Western Railroad established service to Wooddale in 1872. Passengers can still view Wooddale Covered Bridge from a train operated by the WWRR, now a nonprofit historical railroad.

Beginning service in 1872, the WWRR originally hauled passengers and freight along Red Clay Creek between Landenberg, Pennsylvania, and the port of Wilmington, Delaware. The many mills along Red Clay Creek, as well as White Clay Creek, and the popular Victorian-era resort at Brandywine Springs made for a profitable line until the Great Depression. Thereafter, the line was successively shortened down to the current 10-mile track, which was purchased in 1982 by the Historic Red Clay Valley, Inc., which owns and operates the WWRR.

The railroad's 10-mile track runs from Greenbank to Hockessin along the path of Red Clay Creek. The line suffered heavy damage from floods caused by Hurricane Floyd in 1999 and Tropical Storm Henri in 2003, the latter of which reduced the operable route to 2 miles. Fortunately, both the historical railroad and the covered bridge have been rebuilt.

Wooddale Covered Bridge in 2009, 2013, and 2009. *Photos courtesy of Jim and Gloria Smedley, ©2009–2013*

A Pair of Delaware Covered-Bridge Stringers

Westminster Covered Bridge

Location: Westminster residential development, Hockessin, Delaware

Body of Water Crossed: Hyde Run, a tributary of Red Clay Creek

Description: This small red stringer crosses a small creek in the heart of a residential neighborhood.

Open to Vehicular Traffic: Yes

The Covered Bridge at Covered Bridge Farms

Location: Covered Bridge / Bridle Brook Lanes, Covered Bridge Farms development, Newark, Delaware

Body of Water Crossed: Christina Creek

Description: This small, red stringer stands at the entrance to a housing development off Wedgewood Road.

Open to Vehicular Traffic: Yes

DRIVING TOUR
OF THE
COVERED BRIDGES

The following are suggested directions to maximize your covered-bridge exposure. The full tour will travel through five counties in three states. This tour does not include the two covered bridges on private property owned by the Brandywine Conservancy. By no means is this tour the only or optimal path to see the bridges. Unless you start early, end late, encounter no traffic, and make zero stops (and you'll surely want to get out of the car to see the bridges up close), it's not likely that the tour can be completed in one trip.

This tour is set up to begin with the covered bridges in the central part of Chester County in a clockwise loop format, with the bridges grouped by area, so you can choose where to begin and end the tour. Take your time to stop and see the bridges and imagine what life was like when they were built.

Please exercise caution when touring the covered bridges, observe all traffic laws, obey the bridge traffic constraints, help protect the integrity of the covered bridges, and respect the rights of neighboring property owners as you enjoy the scenic landscapes. The tours will take you on some narrow roads, several of which are gravel and can be rough in wet weather (detours for paved roads, where applicable, are noted). Watch for pedestrians and deer, especially in wooded areas and around Valley Forge National Historical Park. The author makes no guarantees that the bridges or roads leading to them will be open, since both are subject to the whims of Mother Nature and government bureaucracy.

Most of the covered bridges are open to vehicular traffic, but they can accommodate only a single lane of traffic. Grab your camera and enjoy the tour!

Central Chester County Covered Bridges

(Brandywine and Doe Run areas)

From the Chatham area, follow Route 841 to the intersection with Route 82 in Doe Run village. Turn left to follow Route 82 North, and take the second road to the right, Covered Bridge Road. Follow it to the intersection with Frog Hollow Road, where you will find **Speakman No. 1 Covered Bridge**. Follow Frog Hollow Road across Speakman No. 1 and follow it to a T with Strasburg Road. Turn right onto Strasburg Road. After traveling through Mortonville and just before Romansville and Stargazer's Village, you will come to a roundabout (traffic circle). Go through the roundabout, turning off onto Shadyside Road. This is a winding and hilly road that can be difficult to follow through its curves and intersections. Shadyside ends at a traffic light on Downingtown Pike (US Route 322). You will see the next covered bridge across the pike, but it's on a one-way street coming at you. To access the bridge, turn right onto Route 322 South. Take the first left onto Skelp Level Road (across from the electrical towers). At the four-way stop, turn left onto Harmony Hill Road and follow it to **Gibson's Covered Bridge**.

Northern Chester County Covered Bridges

(Eagle, Kimberton, and Valley Forge areas)

From Gibson's, if you can drive over the bridge (it was closed for repairs in September 2021 but reopened in January 2022), turn right onto Downingtown Pike (Route 322 North) and follow it into Downingtown. Cross straight over Lancaster Avenue (Business US 30 or Wallace Avenue) and follow PA Route 282 to the US Route 30 bypass. Take Route 30 east toward Exton. Take the exit for PA Route 113 North toward Lionville. Turn left onto Pottstown Pike (PA Route 100 North) and follow it toward Eagle.

If you cannot drive over Gibson's, retrace your path to Skelp Level Road. Turn left onto Skelp Level Road to Boot Road. Turn right and follow Boot Road to Pottstown Pike (PA Route 100 North) and follow it toward Eagle.

As you enter the village of Eagle, stay to the right to follow Graphite Mine Road. **Larkin's Mill Covered Bridge** will be in front of you on the right, just past the intersection with Station Mine Road.

Turn into Byers Station development and turn around so you come back out to Graphite Mine Road. Turn left and follow to Byers Road, where you'll take a left. Follow Byers Road west to PA Route 401 / Conestoga Road. Turn left onto Route 401. Take the second right onto Messner Road (this is a narrow road). You'll come to a stop sign at a T in the road. Turn left onto Horseshoe Trail and follow for a short while until you come to Hollow Road. Turn right onto Hollow Road and follow it to **Hall's/Sheeder's Covered Bridge.**

Cross the bridge and continue on Hollow Road (which becomes Sheeder Road) to Hallmans Mill Road (opposite Wade Drive) and turn right. Turn left onto Hoffecker Road, then a quick right onto Lucas Road. At the stop sign, turn right onto Seven Stars Road. Follow Seven Stars Road and drive across **Kennedy Covered Bridge**.

Follow Seven Stars Road to the four-way stop with Hares Hill Road. Turn left onto Hares Hill. Shortly after you cross the steel bridge, turn right onto Camp Council Road. At the stop sign, you'll see **Rapps Dam Covered Bridge** on your right. If the bridge is open to traffic (it was closed in 2021 but reopened by January 2022), turn right onto Rapps Dam Road and cross the bridge (there is parking in the recreation area on the other side of the bridge). To get to the next bridge, follow Rapps Dam Road south to Route 113. Turn left onto Route 113 North toward Phoenixville. Turn right onto Route 23 East and follow through Phoenixville.

If the bridge is closed to traffic (it was as of September 2021), turn left to follow Rapps Dam Road to Route 23. Turn right onto Route 23 and follow through Phoenixville.

Route 23 is known as Nutt Road, then Valley Forge Road. Follow Route 23 / Valley Forge Road to the intersection with Valley Creek Road (PA Route 252). Turn right onto Valley Creek Road (Route 252). Turn right onto Yellow Springs Road and cross over **Knox-Valley Forge Dam Covered Bridge**.

Eastern Chester County Covered Bridge

(Media, Delaware County area)

From Knox-Valley Forge bridge, follow Yellow Springs Road to Mill Road, and turn left onto Mill Road. Turn right onto Duportail Road. Turn left onto Swedesford Road West and follow it to Bearhill Paoli Road (Route 252). Turn right onto PA 252 South and follow it toward Newtown Square into Delaware County. Stay in the right lane. Turn right onto Goshen Road and follow it to **Bartram's Covered Bridge**.

New Castle County, Delaware, Covered Bridges

(including two stringers in the White Clay Creek Preserve
in southeastern Chester County)

From Bartram's, follow Goshen Road west. It will become Strasburg Road. Follow it to PA Route 3 West. Take Route 3 West to Route 202 South. Follow 202 south into Delaware. Shortly after you cross into Delaware, you'll come to a traffic light with Beaver Valley Road and Naamans Road (DE Route 92). Turn right onto Beaver Valley Road. Take the first left onto Ramsey Road. At the Y, stay to the right to follow Ramsey Road. The road will become Creek Road and follow along Brandywine Creek. Follow Creek Road to the stop sign, and **Smith's Covered Bridge** will be on your left.

Turn left and cross the bridge. Follow Smith's Bridge Road to the four-way stop. Go straight across onto Center Meeting Road. Then take a right onto Route 52 North / Kennett Pike. Take the first road left onto Owls Nest Road. At the four-way stop, turn right onto Old Kennett Road, then the first left onto Way Road and follow it to Route 82. Turn right onto Route 82 and then take the first left onto Barley Mill Road, which will bring you to **Ashland Covered Bridge**. [**Alternate route:** If Way Road is closed, continue on Old Kennett Road to Ashland Clinton Road on your left.

Follow Ashland Clinton Road to the stop sign at Creek Road. Turn left onto Creek Road, then take the first right (a sharp turn) onto Barley Mill Road and follow it to Ashland Covered Bridge.] Note that, despite its rural setting, this is a high-traffic bridge.

Cross over Ashland and follow Barley Mill Road to Rolling Mill Road, which will be on your right. Follow Rolling Mill to **Wooddale Covered Bridge** on the right.

Continue on Rolling Mill Road to DE Route 48 / Lancaster Pike. Turn right onto Route 48 and get in the left turning lane to take the left onto Hercules Road. At the traffic light with Route 41 / Newport-Gap Pike, turn right. Then make the first right turn into the Westminster development on Cheltenham. Turn left on the first road, Heritage, then right on Amblerside to **Westminster Covered Bridge**. Follow Amblerside to Cheltenham and turn left, onto Cheltenham. Then turn right onto Hercules and follow it to the light at Route 41.

Drive straight across over Route 41. The road becomes Mill Creek Road. Follow it to Route 7. Turn right onto Route 7 and follow to the intersection with Little Baltimore Road. [**Alternate route:** After you cross McKennans Church Road, Mill Creek becomes a winding and hilly road. If you prefer a less winding road, follow Mill Creek to Stoney Batter, turn left on Stoney Batter, and follow it to Route 7 / Limestone Road.]

From Route 7, turn left onto Little Baltimore Road and follow it into Pennsylvania. After you cross the state line, take the first left onto Broad Run Road. After you cross the third open bridge, the road will form a Y at the entrance to White Clay Creek Preserve. Stay to the left for London Tract Road. You'll see woods on your left—turn in for the parking area for the preserve. There you'll see one of the **White Clay Creek Preserve stringer covered bridges** at the opening of the Penn-Del Trail there.

From the parking area, turn left onto London Tract Road. After you cross an open concrete bridge, turn left to stay on London Tract (straight becomes Glen Road). You'll come to a stop sign at the London Tract Meeting House. Take a left, then a quick right (essentially, it's straight across) onto South Bank Road and follow it up the hill to the stop sign at Route 896. Turn left on Route 896 southbound.

From here, you can visit the second stringer in the White Clay Creek Preserve, but that involves driving down a rough road and walking the park trail to the bridge. To see the stringer, take the first road to the left, Chambers Rock Road, and follow it to Arc Corner Road. This will be a right turn at the crest of a small hill, so it's easy to miss. Arc Corner Road is unpaved and can be rough. Follow it to the parking lot. Walk east on the trail (the former extension of the road) and you'll come to the second **White Clay Creek Preserve stringer**.

Retrace your path back to Chambers Rock Road. Turn left and follow it to Route 896. Turn left onto 896 and follow it into Delaware. After you pass the White Clay Creek State Park on your left, turn right onto Wedgewood Road. Turn left onto Covered Bridge Lane, where you'll see the **Covered Bridge Farms stringer** ahead of you.

Cecil County, Maryland, Covered Bridges

Cross the Covered Bridge Farms bridge and follow the roads in the triangle to turn around back through the bridge and turn left onto Wedgewood. At the stop sign with Route 273 West / Telegraph Road, turn right onto Route 273 west. At the roundabout, turn right onto Appleton Road. You'll cross under an overpass, and shortly thereafter on the left will be Black Bridge Road and the entrance to the Fair Hill Natural Resources Management Area. Follow Black Bridge Road (this can be a rough road) through the NRMA to **Foxcatcher Covered Bridge**.

[**Option to avoid the rough road**: instead of turning onto Appleton, continue straight on Route 273 toward Fair Hill. Turn left on Entrance Road No. 3 (after an overpass and right at the beginning of the fairgrounds), then left and cross the bridge over Route 273. Turn right onto Tawes Drive and follow it to **Foxcatcher Farm Covered Bridge**. After visiting the bridge, retrace your path back to Route 273 and turn left to head west.]

From Foxcatcher Farm Covered Bridge, follow the road through the park to the stop sign. Either turn left and follow the road out to Route 273 (where you'll turn left to head west) or, for a scenic drive, turn right onto Training Center Drive, which will take you past the facilities used to train the famed horse Barbaro. At the stop sign you will be at Route 213. Turn left and follow to Route 273, where you'll take a right turn to head west.

Follow 273 West to traffic light with Route 272. Turn left and follow 272 South toward North East. Shortly after you pass Warburton Road on your left, **Gilpin's Falls Covered Bridge** will be on the left side of the road, right before you reach Cecil College. There is a small parking area just after the bridge. Turn around and retrace your path on DE 272 North. Follow 272 into Pennsylvania.

Southern Chester County Covered Bridges

(Oxford area)

Traveling north on Route 272, at the first intersection in Pennsylvania, turn right onto Chrome Road. It will become State Road, which you should follow to Hickory Hill Road. Turn right onto Hickory Hill Road and follow it to **Glen Hope Covered Bridge**.

Cross the bridge and follow the road (into Maryland) to the intersection with Blake Road. Turn left and follow Blake Road to Route 472 (Lewisville Road).

Alternate to visit site of Rudolph and Arthur Covered Bridge: In September 2021, the remnants of Hurricane Ida washed away the Rudolph and Arthur Covered Bridge.

If the Rudolph and Arthur bridge is replaced: From Blake Road, turn right onto Route 472 and follow it to Lewisville. At the stop with 841, turn left onto 841 North. You'll come to a stop sign at a Y with Chesterville Road. Turn left onto Lewisville Road. At the next stop sign, turn left onto Camp Bonsul Road and follow it down to the bridge. Cross the bridge and continue on Camp Bonsul to the stop sign. At the stop sign, go straight across onto Route 472 west. After you cross State Road, take the first road to the right, Kings Row Road. Follow it to **Linton Stevens Covered Bridge.**

If the Rudolph and Arthur bridge is not replaced and you cannot drive across: You'll need to retrace your steps back to Lewisville Road. Before you get to Lewisville Road, turn left on Thunder Hill Road and follow it to the intersection with Saginaw Road and Kings Row Road. Turn left onto Kings Row Road and follow it to **Linton Stevens Covered Bridge.** Drive through the bridge and follow Kings Row Road to Route 472.

Alternate to go straight to Linton Stevens Covered Bridge: From Blake Road, turn left onto Route 472, heading east toward Oxford. The road will make a sharp left (Camp Bonsul Road will go off to the right, which can be followed to the site of the Rudolph and Arthur Covered Bridge site). Follow Route 472 to the stop sign at State Road. Continue on Route 472. Take the next right onto Kings Row Road and follow it to **Linton Stevens Covered Bridge.** Pass through the bridge and follow the road to the stop sign with Saginaw Road. Turn left onto Saginaw and then right at the next stop sign back onto Route 472 West.

Follow Route 472 west through Oxford. After you cross over Route 1, take the third road to the left, Street Road. Follow it to the T at Forge Road. Turn right and follow Forge Road to the **Pine Grove Covered Bridge.**

Octoraro Covered Bridges

(Southwestern Chester and Southeastern Lancaster Counties)

Go through Pine Grove bridge and you're on Ashville Road in Lancaster County. Follow it to King Pen Road and take a right (brick posts mark the road) onto King Pen. Follow King Pen to the **White Rock Forge Covered Bridge.**

Cross the bridge and follow Academy Road. As you come up the first hill, stay to the right at the Y in the road to stay on Academy Road, which you'll follow into the village of Union. At the stop sign in Union, turn right onto Street Road and follow to the stop sign at Route 472.

Turn left onto Route 472. After the village of Kirkwood, take the second road to the right, Pumping Station Road. At the stop sign, cross over Bartville Road, continuing on Pumping Station. Turn right onto Dry Wells Road, then at the bottom of a hill, turn right onto Hollow Road. Follow Hollow Road to **Jackson's Mill Covered Bridge**.

Cross the bridge and you're on Mt. Pleasant Road. At the stop sign, turn right on Dry Wells Road and follow it to the village of Nine Points. Turn right onto Route 896 / Georgetown Road, then take the quick first left onto Noble Road. After a short while, you'll pass the Freedom Life Christian Center on your left, and then the road will curve left at a horse farm (a round-top barn will be ahead of you). At that curve, stay to the right to travel onto Creek Road, then take the first right to stay on Creek Road, which will take you to **Mercer's Mill Road** (don't turn left to stay on Creek Road; go straight on what becomes Bailey's Crossroads to the bridge).

Cross the bridge and you're on Bailey's Crossroads Road. Follow it to the stop sign. Go left onto Highland Road and follow it to Route 41. Turn right and follow past the intersection with Route 10. Turn left onto Route 926 and follow 926 to the Chatham area, where there is a four-way stop with Route 841. Turn left onto Route 841 North and follow it to Doe Run.

ACKNOWLEDGMENTS

This book grew out of two articles I wrote on covered bridges that were published in the *Chester County Press*. I thank Randall Lieberman and his staff for their support regarding those articles and this project.

I have to express my appreciation and gratitude to all the local historical commissions and associations, including the Octoraro Art Association and the Upper Oxford Township Historical Commission. It's hard to live in an area with so many historic resources and not become curious and protective of them. The passion and dedication I see in the members of local historical and community associations inspire me to learn more about our local heritage and share it with others. Thank you for providing me with information and support. Like the covered bridges, many historic resources have been, and will be, lost to the tests of time. But they will not disappear so long as there are people like you to record them for posterity.

Thanks to all who provided information about the covered bridges. The Chester County Historical Society's newspaper-clipping files and other collections are an invaluable resource.

My appreciation extends to Al Gaspari, codes officer of Upper Uwchlan Township, for sharing information about the history and rehabilitation of Larkin's Mill Covered Bridge. Congratulations to the locals of the Marsh Creek area whose efforts saved the bridge from destruction in the 1970s and then led to bringing it back to glory after three decades of degradation in a lonely field.

Thanks to the Theodore Burr Covered Bridge Society of Pennsylvania and the National Society for the Preservation of Covered Bridges, both truly great resources for learning about and preserving covered bridges. Special thanks to Jim Smedley for assistance with photographs for this book.

I am grateful to Earl Simmers of the Gilpin's Falls Covered Bridge Committee in Cecil County, Maryland. I enjoyed meeting you by chance at the bridge and learning about the rehabilitation. Thanks to your committee, the bridge will be cherished by future generations of Cecil County and beyond.

Thanks to my parents for introducing me to the covered bridges. I remember occasional family road trips that involved back-roads detours through Pine Grove and Jackson's Mill Covered Bridges. You've kept the memory of Bell Bank and Newcomer's alive with your stories. Thanks to my mother for stocking my library of covered-bridge books. Thanks to my father for accompanying me on long, usually fruitless, driving tours trying to find the bridges by using outdated map tours. It was fun to see not only where the bridges still stand, but where they once stood.

To my husband, Edward, thank you for sharing me with this project and serving as my sounding board. Some of my favorite memories are driving through covered bridges and charging you the toll of a kiss to cross it. I hope to see many more "kissing" bridges with you. To Joe and Kevin, expect many more "boring" trips to visit these timeless treasures. My hope is that someday you'll remember them as interesting.

To Mary, thank you for being my constant cheerleader and unbending supporter.

To Sharon; Joseph, Eli, and my fellow Wondrous Writers; and Theresa and the Springfield Museum writing group: thanks for listening to and supporting me as I crossed many rivers, over calm and rough waters, on my journey to turn a dream into reality.

Most of all, thanks to those who appreciate covered bridges for the rich resources they are, and strive to preserve them for future generations to enjoy.

Groundhog Day festivities near the White Rock Forge Covered Bridge in 2010. *Photo by Sara Beth A. R. Kohut*

BIBLIOGRAPHY AND SOURCES

Alan Gaspari, telephone interview by the author, December 17, 2009.

Allen, Richard Sanders. *Covered Bridges of the Middle Atlantic States: Their Illustrated History in War and Peace*. Brattleboro, VT: Stephen Greene, 1959.

Allen, Richard Sanders. *Covered Bridges of the Northeast*. Mineola, NY: Dover, 2004.

"A New Cover for an Old Bridge." *Southern Lancaster County Chronicle*, March 20, 2006.

Associated Press. "Barbaro Euthanized after Lengthy Battle." NBC Sports, January 29, 2007.

Bedford County Visitors Bureau. *Bedford County Covered Bridges*. Bedford, PA: Bedford County Visitors Bureau, ca. 2004.

Billett, Don. *A Guide to the Beautiful and Historic Covered Bridges of Lancaster County, Pennsylvania*. Mt. Joy, PA: 2006.

Brandywine Conservancy Environmental Management Center. "The Laurels Preserve." Chadds Ford, PA: Brandywine Conservancy, 2006.

Brown, Alberta W. "Covered Bridges." *Chester County Day News*, October 5, 1963.

Burghart, F. J., and S. Kuncevich. "The Covered Bridge." *Philadelphia Inquirer Magazine*, November 14, 1969.

Caravan, Jill. *American Covered Bridges: A Pictorial History*. Philadelphia: Running Press Book, 1995.

Carter, Annette. "The Covered Bridges of Chester County." *Sunday Bulletin Magazine*, May 27, 1962.

Caswell, William S., Jr., ed. *World Guide to Covered Bridges*. 8th ed. Concord, NH: National Society for the Preservation of Covered Bridges, 2021.

Charles X. Carlson Octoraro Art Association. "Brief History of the OAA." Accessed January 27, 2010. http://www.octoraroart.org.

"Chester County's Covered Bridges." *Philadelphia Inquirer*, July 3, 1966.

Chester County Tourist Bureau. *Bridges of Chester County: Visitors Guide Map of Chester County and Brandywine Valley*. West Chester, PA: Chester County Tourist Bureau, 1982.

Chester County Tourist Promotion Bureau in cooperation with the Planning Commission. "Covered Bridges in Chester County Pennsylvania." 1964.

Church, Johanna. "Touring Chester County's Covered Bridges." *Township Voice*, September 19, 1991.

Collins, Kenneth W. *Covered Bridges of Lancaster County, Pennsylvania*. Ephrata, PA: CPC / Science Press, 2002.

Commonwealth of Pennsylvania, Department of Conservation and Natural Resources. "White Clay Creek Preserve." Accessed January 9, 2023. https://www.dcnr.pa.gov/StateParks/FindAPark/WhiteClayCreekPreserve/Pages/default.aspx.

Commonwealth of Pennsylvania, Pennsylvania Historical and Museum Commission, and Pennsylvania Department of Transportation. *Historic Highway Bridges in Pennsylvania*. 1986.

Conn, D. George, Christopher P. Driscoll, Eric D. Gerst, and Doug P. Humes. *Bartram Covered Bridge: Spanning History*. Newtown Square, PA: Newtown Square Historical Preservation Society, 2010.

Conwill, Joseph D. *Covered Bridges*. Oxford: Shire, 2014.

"Covered Bridge Happenings: Pennsylvania—Speakman No. 1 Bridge Repaired after Five[-]Year Closure." *The Newsletter* (National Society for the Preservation of Covered Bridges), Winter 2016/17.

"Covered Spans Take Traveler Back in History." *Philadelphia Inquirer*, June 23, 1961.

"Damage to Bridges." *Daily Local News*, May 16, 1968.

Delaware Department of Transportation. "Apparent Low Bidder Announced for Covered Bridge on Smith's Bridge Road Over the Brandywine Creek." Press release, March 18, 2002.

Delaware Department of Transportation. "Ashland Covered Bridge Ceremony Celebration of Bridge Completion." Press release, June 24, 2008.

Delaware Department of Transportation. "Construction Start Delayed on Smith's Bridge." Press release, July 25, 2002.

Delaware Department of Transportation. "Construction to Start on Covered Bridge on Smith Bridge Road over the Brandywine Creek." Press release, July 19, 2002.

Delaware Department of Transportation. "Low Bidder Announced for the Reconstruction of the Wooddale Covered Bridge over Red Clay Creek." Press release, June 26, 2007.

Delaware Department of Transportation. "Low Bidder Announced for Rehabilitation of Red Clay Creek Covered Bridge." Press release, September 5, 2007.

Delaware Department of Transportation. "Public Invited to Workshop for Replacement of Wooddale Covered Bridge." Press release, May 1, 2006.

Delaware Department of Transportation. "Road Closure Needed for Part of Smith's Bridge Construction." Press release, November 20, 2002.

Delaware Department of Transportation. "Smith Bridge Road Closed for Covered-Bridge Replacement." Press release, August 16, 2002.

Delaware Department of Transportation. "Smith Bridge Reopened." Press release, January 13, 2003.

Delaware Department of Transportation. "Traffic Alert—Ashland Covered Bridge and Barley Mill Road to Temporarily Re-open." Press release, January 18, 2008.

Delaware Department of Transportation. "Traffic Alert—Ashland Covered Bridge Damaged by Hit and Run." Press release, October 17, 2008.

Delaware Department of Transportation. "Traffic Alert—Barley Mill Road to Close as Improvements Are Made to Ashland Covered Bridge." Press release, November 29, 2007.

Delaware Department of Transportation. "Traffic Alert—Closure of Rolling Mill Road for the Reconstruction of Wooddale Covered Bridge." Press release, August 31, 2007.

Delaware Department of Transportation. "Traffic Alert—Update: Ashland Covered Bridge Re-opens One Month Early." Press release, May 15, 2008.

Delaware Department of Transportation. "Traffic Alert—Wooddale Covered Bridge Re-opens." Press release, December 17, 2008.

"DelDOT Officials Honored for Bridge (from Staff Reports, *The News Journal*, Jan. 31, 2003)." Delaware Department of Transportation Media Gallery, State of Delaware, 2009.

Earl Simmers, interview by the author, January 16, 2010.

East Pikeland Township. "A General East Pikeland History." Accessed January 9, 2023. https://www.eastpikeland.org.

East Vincent Township. "The Covered Bridges of East Vincent." Accessed January 9, 2023. https://www.eastvincent.org/indexasp?SEC=1ED3D073-0843-44FC-9B33-9962884D2529.

Elk Township. "Elk Township History." Accessed January 9, 2023. https://www.elktownship.org/about/history/.

Evans, Benjamin D., and June R. Evans. *Pennsylvania's Covered Bridges: A Complete Guide*. Pittsburgh, PA: University of Pittsburgh Press, 1993.

Evans, Benjamin D., and June R. Evans. *Pennsylvania's Covered Bridges: A Complete Guide*. 2nd ed. Pittsburgh, PA: University of Pittsburgh Press, 2001.

Falk, Henry C. "Bridges of Pennsylvania: Delaware County." *Covered Bridge Topics*, Spring 1988.

Fitzcharles, Margaret. "Supervisors Seek Repair of Covered Bridge." *Daily Local News*, December 30, 2002.

Fuller, Roy R. "Exploring the Covered Bridges of Chester County." *Upper Main Line News*, October 23, 1953; October 30, 1953; and November 6, 1953.

Gaintner, J. Richard. "Covered Wooden Bridges." In *Free Official Pennsylvania Dutch Guide-Book*. Lancaster, PA: Pennsylvania Dutch Tourist Bureau, 1962.

Gilkyson, Phoebe H. "Chester County Famous for Bridge Burners." *Daily Republican*, November 25, 1962.

Gregory Penny, Pennsylvania Department of Transportation, telephone interview by the author, December 17, 2009.

Greiner, Kay. [Untitled]. *Downingtown Archive*, October 16, 1968.

Historic Red Clay Valley. "Our History." Wilmington & Western Railroad. Accessed January 9, 2023. https://www.wwrr.com/about/history.aspx.

Horst, Melvin J., and Elmer Lewis Smith. *Covered Bridges of Pennsylvania Dutchland*. 20th ed. Lebanon, PA: Applied Arts Publishers, 1997.

James, Arthur E. *Covered Bridges of Chester County*. Kennett Square, PA: KNA Press, 1976.

Jan Bowers, Chester County director of Department of Facilities, telephone interview by the author, January 21, 2022.

Krekeler, Brenda. *Covered Bridges Today*. Canton, OH: Daring, 1989.

Lehigh Valley: Lehigh Valley Convention and Visitors Bureau. "Tracking Covered Bridges in the Lehigh Valley: A Self Guided Tour." n.d.

Magee, D. F. "The Old Wooden Covered Bridges of the Octoraro." Papers read before the Lancaster County Historical Society, Lancaster, PA, September 7, 1923.

Maryland Department of Natural Resources. "Fair Hill NMRA." Accessed January 9, 2023. https://dnr.maryland.gov/publiclands/pages/central/fairhill.aspx.

Maye, Fran. "Resident Hailed for Alerting Police to Bridge Damaged by Driver." *Daily Local News*, November 4, 2011.

Mueller, Dave. "Pessimism Stalks Return of Bridge." *Daily Local News*, March 20, 1979.

National Register of Historic Places, Ashland Bridge, Ashland, New Castle County, Delaware, National Register #73000506.

National Register of Historic Places, Bartram's Covered Bridge, Media, Chester and Delaware Counties, Pennsylvania, National Register #80003462.

National Register of Historic Places, Doe Run Village Historic District, West Marlborough Township, Chester County, Pennsylvania, National Register #85002349.

National Register of Historic Places, Gibson's Covered Bridge, Downingtown, Chester County, Pennsylvania, National Register #80003456.

National Register of Historic Places, Gilpin's Falls Covered Bridge, North East, Cecil County, Maryland, National Register #08001125.

National Register of Historic Places, Glen Hope Covered Bridge, West Grove, Chester County, Pennsylvania, National Register #80003472.

National Register of Historic Places, Hall's, Sheeder Covered Bridge, Chester Springs, Chester County, Pennsylvania, National Register #73001600.

National Register of Historic Places, Kennedy Covered Bridge, Kimberton, Chester County, Pennsylvania, National Register #74001770.

National Register of Historic Places, Larkin Covered Bridge, Downingtown, Chester County, Pennsylvania, National Register #80003458.

National Register of Historic Places, Linton Stevens Covered Bridge, New London, Chester County, Pennsylvania, National Register #80003466.

National Register of Historic Places, Mercer's Mill Covered Bridge, Atglen, Chester and Lancaster Counties, Pennsylvania, National Register #80003509.

National Register of Historic Places, Pine Grove Covered Bridge, Oxford, Chester and Lancaster Counties, Pennsylvania, National Register #80003521.

National Register of Historic Places, Rapps Covered Bridge, Mont Clare, Chester County, Pennsylvania, National Register #73001608.

National Register of Historic Places, Rudolph & Arthur Covered Bridge, West Grove, Chester County, Pennsylvania, National Register #80003473.

National Register of Historic Places, Speakman #1 Covered Bridge, Modena, Chester County, Pennsylvania, National Register #80003464.

National Register of Historic Places, Speakman #2, Mary Ann Pyle Bridge, Modena, Chester County, Pennsylvania, National Register #80003465.

National Register of Historic Places, Valley Forge National Historical Park, Norristown, Chester County, Pennsylvania, National Register #66000657.

National Register of Historic Places, White Rock Forge Covered Bridge, Kirkwood, Lancaster County, Pennsylvania, National Register #80003522.

National Register of Historic Places, Wooddale Bridge, Wooddale, New Castle County, Delaware, National Register #73000552.

National Register of Historic Places Inventory—Nomination Form, Covered Bridges of Chester County Thematic Resources, Chester County, Pennsylvania. Accessed January 9, 2023. https://catalog.archives.gov/id/71992694.

National Register of Historic Places Inventory—Nomination Form, Covered Bridges of Lancaster County Thematic Resources, Lancaster County, Pennsylvania. Accessed January 9, 2023. https://catalog.archives.gov/id/71993253.

National Register of Historic Places Inventory—Nomination Form, Gilpin's Falls Historic District, Cecil County, Maryland, 1978.

"News of Old Covered Bridges: Maryland—Gilpin's Falls Bridge." *The Newsletter* (National Society for the Preservation of Covered Bridges), Winter 2010.

"News of Old Covered Bridges: Pennsylvania—Rapps Dam Covered Bridge." *The Newsletter* (National Society for the Preservation of Covered Bridges), Winter 2012.

Township of Newtown Square, Delaware County, Pennsylvania. "Bartram Bridge Joint Preservation Commission." Accessed January 9, 2023. https://www.newtowntownship.org/220/Bartram-Bridge-Joint-Commission.

Nicolas Janberg's Structurae: International Database and Gallery of Structures. "Gilpin's Falls Covered Bridge." Accessed January 9, 2023. https://structurae.net/en/structures/gilpin-s-falls-covered-bridge.

"One by One the Old Covered Bridges Go." *Daily Local News*, August 3, 1963.

Pendleton, Philip E. *Architectural Resources Survey, Smiths Bridge Road Improvements, New Castle County, Delaware*. Prepared for the Delaware Department of Transportation. East Orange, NJ: Cultural Resource Group, Louis Berger & Associates, 1999.

Pennsylvania State Police. Public Information Release Report, Incident No. J02-1084736, November 16, 2005.

Peters, Richard. *A Statistical Account of the Schuylkill Permanent Bridge, Communicated to the Philadelphia Society of Agriculture, 1806*. Philadelphia: Reprint of Jane Aitken, 1807.

Pfingsten, Bill. "Gilpin's Falls Covered Bridge." Accessed January 9, 2023. http://www.hmdb.org/marker.asp?marker=1692.

"Picturesque Covered Bridges Disappearing from Pa. Scenes." *Right of Way*, December 1953.

Pierce, Phillip C., Robert L. Brungraber, Abba Lichtenstein, and Scott Sabol. *Covered Bridge Manual*. Publication FHWA-HRT-04-098. McLean, VA: United States Department of Transportation, Federal Highway Administration, 2005.

"Pine Grove Span Re-opens." *Lancaster New Era*, August 25, 2008, B5.

Powell, Pam. "Covered Bridges Connect Past with Present." *Daily Local News, Chester County Living*, December 11, 2005.

Rachel Sangree, interview by the author, January 16, 2010.

Rathmell, James K., Jr. "Delaware County, Pennsylvania Covered Bridge Starred in Movie." *Covered Bridge Topics*, October 1958.

Robinson, Ryan. "Man Charged after Driving into Covered Bridge." *Intelligencer Journal*, March 20, 2010.

"The Roll Call of Our Ill-Fated Covered Bridges." *Daily Local News*, May 31, 1967.

Rossomando, John. "Before the Lake." *Daily Local News*, May 6, 2006.

Rossomando, John. "Covered-Bridge Dedication Planned." *Daily Local News*, June 23, 2006.

Sloane, Eric. *American Barns and Covered Bridges*. Mineola, NY: Dover, 2002.

Smedley, Jim. "Maryland Covered Bridges." Accessed January 9, 2023. http://www.mdcovered-bridges.com/index.html.

Theodore Covered Bridge Society of Pennsylvania. "Smith's Bridge Damaged by Tractor Trailer." *Pennsylvania Crossings*, Summer 2021.

Umble, Chad. "Recovered Bridge." *Lancaster New Era*, July 18, 2008, A1.

Untitled. *Daily Local News*, January 18, 1885; and July 14, 1884.

Weaver, Elinor K. "Visit the Bridges That Span the Years." *Lukens Life*, July-August [year unknown].

Website for Theodore Burr Covered Bridge Society of Pennsylvania. http://www.tbcbspa.com.

Will Truax, interview by the author, January 16, 2010.

Windle, Spencer. *Pictorial History of Chester County Covered Bridges*. Self-published, ca. 1999.

Wright, David W., ed. *World Guide to Covered Bridges*. 7th ed. Hillsboro, NH: National Society for the Preservation of Covered Bridges, 2009.

A native of Oxford, Pennsylvania, Sara Beth A. R. Kohut grew up and continues to live, work, and play within the tristate area featured in her first book, *Crossing under Cover*. During a short stint as a local newspaper reporter, she wrote many articles on local history, including a story on covered bridges that inspired the book. She has volunteered and contributed newsletter articles for the Upper Oxford Township Historical Commission and the Franklin Township Historical Commission.

Sara Beth holds a bachelor's degree in history and political science from Western Maryland College (now known as McDaniel College), where she was elected to Phi Beta Kappa, and a law degree from the University of Pittsburgh, where she served as an editor for, and was first professionally published in, the law review. She is admitted to practice law in Delaware and Pennsylvania and currently runs her own solo practice.

In her free time, Sara Beth enjoys participating in spontaneous (or organized) covered-bridge safaris and working on her next writing project.